Charlotte Carter

D1590198

The Spiritual Hunger of the Modern Child

The Spiritual Hunger of the Modern Child

A Series of Ten Lectures

Claymont Communications
Charles Town, W. Va.

6/01

These lectures were delivered in London in the autumn of 1961 under the auspices of the Institute for the Comparative Study of History, Philosophy and the Sciences. Since that time, there has been little significant change in the emotional and intellectual education of children, and the lectures can be said to speak as directly to the difficulties and problems of parents and teachers as they did twenty-three years ago.

For this reason, and in the hope that they may be of practical use and interest today, Claymont Communications, in cooperation with the Claymont Children's School, has decided to bring the lectures before a wider public in their present form. We are grateful to Elizabeth Bennett for her help and guidance with this project.

The editors would have liked, as an act of courtesy, to have asked permission from the lecturers before publication. After so long an interval, it is of course inevitable that some of them have already left this world, but, though the editors have tried to make contact with those who remain, we have been able to do so in only one instance. It is hoped, therefore, that we are not causing any offense or impropriety in the publication of the lectures, and if we have done so, we make our apologies.

Excerpts from the original program of the lectures will serve as introduction.

THE LECTURERS

The lecturers for this course are all known as speakers, writers, teachers, and specialists in their fields. But above all they have devoted years of their lives to the promotion of deeper understanding in spiritual matters.

Mr. J. G. Bennett, Mathematician, Industrial Scientist, Traveller, and Linguist, is author of *The Crisis in Human Affairs*, *The Dramatic Universe*, and *Concerning Subud*. He has directed the research for the Institute for the Comparative Study of History, Philosophy, and the Sciences for more than thirty years with Gurdjieff and Ouspensky, and was one of the first in the West to enter the Subud movement. Mr. Bennett has studied the problems of spirituality and childhood as they are dealt with in Asia, Europe, and America.

Dr. Mario Montessori has devoted his life to children and their needs. As the closest associate of his mother, Maria Montessori, one of the greatest educationalists of any age, Dr. Montessori is able to speak from experience of the central place that religious piety occupied in her approach to children.

Mr. Clifford John Williams, following ten years as an actor on both sides of the Atlantic, is now a teacher and lecturer in drama and a student of ancient languages. Brought up in the Anglican Church, he joined the Society of Friends some years ago, and is Chairman of the Quaker Fellowship of the Arts.

The Rev. Adam Bittleston was ordained in 1935 as priest in the Christian Community, the religious body founded in 1922 under the guidance of Dr. Rudolf Steiner, for which he has worked successively in Leeds, London, and Edinburgh. In Scotland he has been actively engaged both in the religious education of normal children, and in the care and treatment of those suffering from mental handicap. He is author of *Meditative Prayers for Today*, and has lectured in many countries.

Mr. A. I. Polack, M.A., will tell us how Jewish parents and teachers face our problem. He served in the army during the 1914-1918 war. Afterwards, he became Assistant Master at Taunton School, and then Housemaster at Clifton College. Since 1939 he has been Education Officer at the Council for Christians and Jews. He is co-author, with the Rev. W. W. Simpson, of the book *Jesus in the Background of History*.

Mr. U. Maung Maung Ji was educated in Rangoon, Benares, Madras, London, and Cambridge. He was Founder-President of the All-India Youth League and a close friend of Mahatma Gandhi. Mr. Maung Maung Ji is President of the London Buddhist Vihara Society, Vice-Chairman of the British-Asian and Overseas Socialist Fellowship, and member of other international organizations for the promotion of human welfare. He is a Barrister-at-Law, and has been an international lecturer for the last thirty years.

Father Hugh S. Thwaites has seen life from many angles—as a publicity officer before the war, as an army artillery officer during the war, as a Japanese prisoner-of-war working on the "Railway of Death" in Siam. Brought up in the Church of England, his spiritual search led him to Christian Science and then to Roman Catholicism. On his return to civilian life in 1945, Mr. Thwaites entered the Jesuit noviceship. He is now Vocations Director at Manresa College, and also National Director of the Knights and Handmaids of the Blessed Sacrament, a Eucharistic crusade that concerns itself with the religious life of adolscents.

CONTENTS

Lecture 1

A Survey of the Problem

J.G. Bennett

My duty tonight is to introduce the theme of these
lectures and offer you a general survey of the problem.
I should not, therefore, attempt to answer the question
in the sub-title: "In our relationship with the young,
what must we do to preserve the religious potential that
is latent in every child?" The speakers who are to come
after me will put forward their own answers, and as I
am among them, I shall have my own opportunity to
speak again. You might suppose that my present task
is an easy one, but the truth is that there is as much
confusion of thought as to what children really need as to
the means of helping them. The problems of modern
youth are being discussed everywhere, and sincere and
well-meaning people can differ as to the very nature of
the problem.

It seems to me that a large part of the confusion comes
from failing to distinguish between spiritual needs and
psychic needs. Also, we often use the word "religious"
with too much emphasis on the outward forms and too
little regard for the inner content. When we were
choosing the title of this series of lectures, we took the
word "spiritual" in order to make it clear that we were
referring to an intangible and almost incommunicable

part of our experience, and that we were concerned with content rather than form. We hoped that our speakers would help us to trace the source of our troubles and show us how they can be remedied, rather than analyze the symptoms in the form of social unrest, loss of confidence in the future, and the consequent tendency to over-prize immediate and often grossly material satisfactions.

I must, therefore, start by explaining what we mean by the word "spiritual." Such terms as spiritual needs and spiritual life imply that there is a reality that cannot be reached through our senses and which we cannot grasp with our minds. If there is such a reality, it must be impossible to form any picture or image of it, and as our thinking depends upon pictures and images, we cannot think about it. Of course, it is possible to deny a spiritual reality and to assert that all that exists can be seen and touched — if not directly, at least indirectly with the help of instruments such as science has developed. Such a view amounts in one way or another to materialism, for it holds, in effect, that there is no reality that is not material.

You will believe now that in choosing the word "spiritual," we lay down a challenge to those who believe that all real problems can be stated and solved in material terms. You need not agree with us—and we have not asked our speakers if they agree with us—but we do want to make it clear that what we want to examine together is the question whether there really are spiritual as distinct from material needs, and if so, how these needs are to be satisfied. We know well enough that all of us have material needs. Our bodies are material things and they cannot live without food, shelter, and all that we call the "necessities of life." Since spiritual needs cannot be seen and touched, nor even expressed in ordinary language, it is much harder to be sure that there really are such needs and of what they consist.

It is just as necessary to distinguish between the spiritual and the psychic as between the spiritual and the material. By "psychic," I mean all that concerns our subjective life, our consciousness of what is happening to us and of what we are doing. The "psyche" is familiar enough in the word psychology. It is sometimes called the "mind," but we have learned from Freud and Jung to accept the psyche as only partly conscious, and it is best, therefore, to keep to this word to cover all that we mean when we distinguish "mind" from "body." The psyche of man includes his sensations, emotions, imaginations, and thoughts—both conscious and unconscious. This part of man has its needs just as the living organism, the body, needs food, water, air, shelter, exercise, and the rest. When we speak of psychic needs, we refer to the various stimulations that are required to maintain the activity and satisfy the desires of our psyche. Without these stimulations, our psyche would languish and lose its powers, even if the body were to remain alive. Psychic needs are as various as the psyche itself. We have emotional needs and desires. We have mental curiosity. We want stimuli for our imagination. We need to express and assert ourselves. All of these and dozens of others create our psychic hunger, and we cannot live unless it is satisfied. But we must not make the mistake of supposing that all our needs are either organic or psychic. You will see what I mean if you recognize that psychic needs can very often be satisfied by experiences that reach us through our senses— whether it is the sight of beauty, or simple physical comforts and satisfactions, and so on. And our intellectual needs can also, to some extent, be satisfied by learning more about the world in which we live through the use of our senses and through the use of the various instruments by which the power of our senses has been extended so enormously in these last centuries. These kinds of needs and these kinds of satisfactions

relate to what I would call the psychic nature of man.
I will have to say more about that in order to introduce
our subject properly, but for the moment, I only want
to make the distinction between psychic needs and
spiritual needs. Our spiritual needs belong to something
that is quite different from our psychic nature; that is,
from our capacity for feeling, for desiring, for imagining,
for thinking, and so on. They are the needs of the
spiritual man, the "I" that is more truly ourselves than
the psychic apparatus of thought, feeling, and sensation.
And yet these spiritual needs are not remote or only
important for very special people, those whom we call
"spiritual people." I want to show you that the spiritual need really begins with something very simple;
that is, with the need to "belong," the need to have a
place, the need that one's life should have a meaning.
This meaning does not depend just upon ourselves or
just upon our environment, but a meaning which is
stable, which we can turn to in all conditions of life.
For most people, this is even a meaning that will go
beyond life and embrace our existence beyond the
death of this body. What is more, this spiritual need
to "belong," for our life to make sense, cannot be something that is private for each one of us; for obviously,
life cannot make sense in isolation from a greater whole.
Herein lies another important difference between the
spiritual need and the psychic need. Our psychic needs
are very personal: It is my own feelings, my own desires, my own curiosity and interest, my own creative
abilities, my own need for self-expression, that consti-
tute psychic needs. They may even be in conflict with
the needs of other people. Very often, in the satisfaction
of their psychic needs people do disregard the needs,
both psychic and physical, of other people. But it is not
so with the spiritual needs, with the spiritual hunger. The
spiritual hunger, I believe, starts really with this necessity
for us to "belong," to have a place, to feel that we are

not isolated, that there is something beyond our own psyche which is not a stranger to us, which is not outside of us. And this quality in the spiritual need means that it is a need that cannot be satisfied—I was going to say cannot be felt, because I think it is true that it cannot be felt—but it certainly cannot be satisfied except in relation to a Whole, in relation to a reality that is more than ourselves.

This simple spiritual hunger for life to make sense, which also means the need that each one of us should have for a place in something greater, is only the beginning. It is a kind of first stirring of the spiritual need, but there comes with it another need, and that is that we should understand, to some extent, why we are here and why the world is as it is. We have a spiritual need to know why we should or should not do something, why there is a duty to live one way and not another. When we come to that question, we have clearly reached one of the spiritual needs of children. These questions "why" and "why should" must be related to something which they can trust, which they believe in, which makes sense for them. If it is not so, the very idea of duty enters among their other psychic activities, the workings of their feelings and of their minds. All of these can be trained, can be discliplined, can be conditioned, but this does not bring any satisfaction for the inner need. The inner man still needs the assurance that what we do matters, that there are reasons why we should live this way and not in that way. Out of this, "Who am I, and why? What should I do, and why?" there begins to be a spiritual need for contact with a larger reality.

Man at all stages of his development and in every period of history has felt this need to "belong," to be able to turn to a greater reality in which he can trust. Moreover, people have always recognized that this need brings with it obligations that may, and indeed usually do, conflict with the impulses of the psyche. When this combination of need and obligation becomes a factor in the life of an individual, we say that he has a "religious sense." Through religion, our private problems cease to be solely human and are brought into relation with the supreme reality that is God. With this, we begin to gain the conviction that there is a reliable answer to all questions of why and wherefore. We begin to recognize the significance of such a phrase as, "God in whom we live and move and have our being." Such expressions can refer only to the spiritual reality that is beyond the reach of the senses and even beyond the understanding of the mind.

I have tried to define for you a distinction that I believe to be real and important for any right understanding of children and their needs. Some of you may not agree that man has a spiritual as distinct from a psychic nature. Others may go further and deny that there is any sense in distinguishing the psychic from the organic. Whether or not we agree about the facts of human nature, I believe that we shall all find it useful to keep our descriptions clear. There are first, as everyone must agree, organic needs of our animal bodies. Secondly, as most people will admit, there are psychic needs that arise in our thoughts, feelings, and imagination, as well as in the deeper regions of the psyche commonly called the "sub-conscious." Thirdly, some, perhaps most of you, will be ready to accept another reality—that of the spiritual part of our nature. I connect this with the "I" of man, with his will and with the freedom that is his most precious attribute. The spiritual needs are not the needs of any part of me, but those that concern "I myself."

Having made these distinctions, I shall try to state the problem of the "Spiritual Hunger of the Modern Child," and suggest the questions to which we are seeking an answer.

The questions begin from the moment of conception. How far is the future life influenced by heredity and by the psychic condition of the parents when the child is conceived? Evidence is accumulating that suggests that these influences make themselves felt throughout life; but I shall say no more about this at present as it would lead me into suggesting answers rather than questions.

After conception, there are pre-natal influences. These affect the body and the psyche in ways that are very evident during the first months after birth. It seems as if a psyche subject to pre-natal disturbances is deprived of its spiritual needs and enters life with a handicap that only special care will overcome.

I only mention conception and gestation to remind you that the spiritual problem may well arise even before the child is born. This we cannot know from any direct evidence, but I believe that much can be learned from the observation of new-born children. I am convinced that we can verify the reality of the spiritual element in our human nature by observing gestures and sounds made by a new-born child. Most of these can be accounted for as organic reflexes, but there are others that strongly suggest that an inner, spiritual awareness is present. At first there is very little awareness arising from sense perception, and the psyche has little or no content in the shape of memories and habits.

In the program of the lectures, the words, "Heaven lies about us in our infancy!" are quoted from William Wordsworth's poem, "Intimations of Immortality from Recollections of Early Childhood." You may or may not be prepared to admit that there is evidence of a spiritual nature present in children from birth, but you will certainly agree that the child begins to be drawn outwards by the influences of the environment—people and things. From this time onwards, the child begins to show psychic as well as organic needs. These tend to obscure the finer spiritual needs, and the child begins to lose that "other-wordly" quality that is so touching and so mysterious for all who are sensitive to its presence.

As the body grows and develops, so also does the

psyche. We observe the awakening of one part of the psyche after another. At first it is mainly instinct, then come feeling, desire, reaction, and so on. Much later, the life of the imagination and thought begin to form, and by the age of puberty the psychic powers or functions are in full activity.

This psychic growth derives its content mainly through what comes from the outside, and the material which is molded into this new psychic nature is that which has come partly from heredity, partly perhaps from the conditions of conception, partly from other sources of which we are not aware. There begins to be present in the child an unmistakable psychic nature to which we give various names, such as personality, or mind, or soul. It has its own needs. Parents and those surrounding the child are necessarily concerned with the organic needs; with feeding and washing and taking care of the little body. They also try to satisfy the psychic needs— perhaps by teaching, by stimulating and encouraging the development of this psychic nature, very often over-encouraging it. They are often too anxious that the child should walk and speak and learn various skills before someone else's child. They want him to develop well and quickly. All this is stimulating psychic develop- ment, but it is also at the same time withdrawing atten- tion, the inner attention, from the spiritual reality with which the child is still in contact.

What, then, satisfies in the young child this spiritual need to hold on to his own spiritual world? Undoubtedly it is, in the first place, the mother, and then the family. The family life satisfies—or should satisfy—the spiritual need of the child for quite a long time. There is a period in the life of a child when nearly all his spiritual needs, his spiritual hunger, can be satisfied by the family en- vironment; but only on the condition that the family environment does really provide for the spiritual needs, and does not exaggerate out of all proportion the importance of the psychic needs. If that is done, then this child will grow up perhaps with an inordinate psychic hunger, a need for experience, for excitement, for interest, for the satisfaction of all these psychic needs. And then, what is it that happens? These psychic needs begin to become psychic imperatives, necessities; emotional desires, emotional impulses that must be satisfied. For some, the desire for attention, appreciation, and so on becomes a must; for others, the desire for self-expression, self-assertion becomes a must. In due course, various other natural powers develop—especially the sexual powers at puberty. The sexual powers at once open the way for the satisfactions of psychic needs with new intensity, new material, new contributions to the psychic life; and again, all this becomes a must. If there is not at the same time some spiritual satisfaction, some spiritual assurance, there is no balance, there is nothing to counterbalance these psychic hungers. And then we have the kind of situation that we recognize only too well in our present time, the "Why shouldn't I, what is wrong?" We know only too well that attempts to answer these questions either on an organic basis or a psychic basis are unconvincing. They sound especially false to the child, who has not had the awakening of the spiritual consciousness that would enable him to recognize the answers for himself, and would make it quite unnecessary for him either to ask the question or to receive the replies to it.

This raises a point on which I believe that all our speakers will agree, and I would venture to put it down as a fair starting point in the study. The point is that we cannot answer questions about what we ought or ought not to do in terms simply of the results that will ensue. To say, "You ought not to do this because if you do it, you will have such and such an unpleasant result," is right neither for the young child nor for the adolescent, nor even for mankind as a whole. That may seem strange, because in the past it has been usual to present "ought" and "ought not" in terms of reward and punishment. "You ought to do this, because if you do you will be rewarded; you ought not do that, because if you do you will be punished," is clearly a nonsensical statement. The word "ought" might just as well be left out, and one could say, "If you will do this, you will be rewarded; if you do that, you will be punished." The word "ought" has ceased to have any place in the conversation as soon as reward and punishment come in; it has simply reduced the whole action to a natural level and has left the spiritual content out of it.

What is the result of trying to have "morals without ought," or a code of conduct without a sense of spiritual obligation? Unanswerable objections are put forward, as we have seen with this question that has disturbed so many people, of sexual disorder in modern youth. We know quite well that if we say, "You ought not to do this, because you may catch a disease," they answer, "But this is the business of the doctors, it is not my business, the doctor has to see that I do not catch a disease or cure me if I catch it." If we say, "You ought not to do this, because you will bring children into the world you do not want and will not want to care for," the answer is, "That is the business of the state, it is not my business, the state is there to look after everyone, and if I feel no sense of responsibility, then others must take it on." We must recognize that that sort of retort is unanswerable so long as we confine the presentation entirely to the organic and the psychic. If we say, "If you do this, you will be unhappy," they answer, "But if I do, I will also be happy, so let me be happy first, and who knows if I will be unhappy afterwards," and the rest of it. In short, there is in reality no psychic foundation for morality.

If one could go beyond the family into a society that could provide a real spiritual environment, then perhaps one could say that the transition from the early child-life, with the family as the sole environment, to the adolescent life, when society begins to be the environment, could be made smoothly. Then the spiritual needs could be satisfied by the sense of belonging to a society in which the words "ought" and "ought not," and in which the feeling "I belong and I matter," expressed a reality that all could recognize. But our human societies have not yet come to this. I believe that we are in the process of a gradual development, that time will bring human society to the spiritual quality that a great family could have. But if we survey our situation as it is today, we have to admit that not only is the society the adolescent enters not a spiritual society, but even the family is very seldom, in these days, a spiritual environment. The family has become much more a psychic environment. I must make it clear that I include in this all the interest and attachment to material things and the assessment of values in terms of possessions and money and the rest of it that we call "materialism." The whole of this creates a psychic complex, and it is that kind of psychic complex that dominates family life in the very great majority of families in this country and in most parts of the world. So that we have, unfortunately, to go right back and recognize that there is for children a truly spiritual environment only before they are born. As soon as they are born, they already begin to be exposed to an environment which is more organic and psychic than spiritual, and this begins even at the very early stages of family life. Well-meaning parents are often concerned only with stimulating the psychic nature of the child, and do not understand the needs of the spiritual nature.

These spiritual needs are not really such profound things that only people of very saintly character and extraordinary spiritual powers can do anything about. They are largely concerned with such qualities as trustworthiness, sincerity, and truthfulness that create the feeling that, "I am in an environment that I can trust." Once we have that sort of starting point, we are able to go on to something very, very much greater in the sense that we shall be able to trust in God. It is more important that parents should provide an environment of trust for their children than that they should provide a condition of psychic stimulation. They seldom understand this, and much the same applies to each of the different factors that go to make up the needs of our spiritual life.

I have spoken already of the word "ought," which is connected with what we call the "sense of duty." I think you will agree that duty has no meaning except in a spiritual sense. There is no such thing as duty in a psychic sense, because the psyche of man is simply that which reacts in different ways to the inner and outer environment—which is the accumlation of his own experiences, his hereditary and atavistic experiences, the whole that goes to make a human psyche. The spiritual man is really concerned with the word "ought." The problem of "ought," that is, the way duty is understood, arises from the earliest days when a child begins to be able to recognize the differences of behavior of those around him. These experiences can thus be an element in satisfying the spiritual hunger of the child. There are many ways in which this sense that duty is something objective—not merely a whim of the parents, not merely a social convenience, but a spiritual reality—can be presented to children. It is presented somewhat differently, for example, according to the form of religious belief or religious worship. It is presented somewhat differently according to the way in which the spiritual reality is understood, or felt, or lived by the parents themselves. It is therefore important that the parents should live so that their spiritual life demonstrates that duty is a reality for them; otherwise, they cannot produce an environment for the child in which duty can be a satisfaction for his spiritual needs. Therefore, if duty is understood simply as something arbitrary, as a social contract, as a bargain, "If I do this, then I get that," then it is only a psychic understanding of duty. If the obligation to do what is right, to serve the needs of our fellow men, is felt as something that is inherent in man's innermost nature, then it is a satisfaction of the spiritual need and produces a spiritual coherence and a spiritual confidence that redress the balance of the egocentric activities of the psyche.

One last aspect of the spiritual needs is the spiritual need for love. Here, of course, it is most necessary to distinguish between the psychic interpretation of love and the spiritual interpretation. The word love is used for all sorts of conditions of reaction, ranging from organic bodily attraction to the impulses of each of the psychic instruments or psychic powers. There is love of sight, love of sound, love of touch, love of feelings, love of imagination, love of thought, and so on through the whole spectrum of psychic experiences. What is ordinarily called love is simply some twist in that kaleidoscope that combines into some pattern or another, and usually a pattern that is continually changing. These different elements in the psychic experience are what I would call psychic love, or love of the psyche. Spiritual love is something different. It is a participation in the Universal Love, in love as a reality in which all the creation shares. Spiritual love ceases to be my love or your love or anyone else's: it is Love, and all religion teaches us that Love is God.

When we first present this to people who have been accustomed to approach human problems solely in terms of their psychic content, it seems something remote. They find it hard to accept that to perform our duty can be a satisfaction for the deepest part of our nature. I believe that they would see differently if only they understood the distinction between our psychic and our spiritual natures. Here, I think that it is legitimate to go back to look at the new-born child and to see how the spiritual quality of the child is present without there yet being any psychic content or any development of the psychic powers. There is hardly such a thing as even seeing, hearing, or recognizing by touch; there is certainly no formation of the emotional nature, or— less still—anything like imagining or power of image formation, or thought or intellectual activity: And yet there is love. Some people will accept that from the evidence of their own experience, but if not, it still remains that we have to make a distinction between love as a spiritual need and a spiritual satisfaction; love as a psychic need and a psychic satisfaction; and, again, love as an organic need.

This is very important in the relations between parents and children, because if parents are concerned only to establish bonds of psychic love between themselves and the child, then they only stimulate the psyche of the child. This produces a relationship that will afterwards be the cause of many difficulties, because the psyche changes and develops and transforms completely as life goes on. Consequently, its capacity for response also changes. Sometimes parents fail to realize that the relationship on the psychic level cannot remain as it was at this particular or that particular stage of the child's development—and also, incidentally, of their own development—and therefore they expect and make demands. Conversely, the child expects and makes demands which cannot be satisfied because they imply a certain stability and continuity of a part of man that is by its nature neither stable nor continuous: that is, the psychic nature. It does not mean, of course, that what we call emotional love, or the stimulation of emotional attractions between parents and children, is undesirable, nor should we undervalue the intellectual delight of the child that learns or the parent that teaches. These various bonds in the psychic nature have their rightful place, but if the development of the relationship is confined to the psychic field, then there will always be trouble, there will always be difficulty in adjustment. The child will suffer most of all when it is no longer able to be in the kind of relationship that was possible at an earlier stage of his development. This is seen so clearly through a study of the stages of transformation of children between the ages of six and eight, or at the time of puberty. Indeed, it occurs earlier. One sees how the psychic bonds which have been created within one period of life are no longer valid at another period, and the adjustment is sometimes not effectively made. But much worse is that something remains starved, both for the parents and for the children, and the capacity for the spiritual relationship of love is not satisfied. That relationship is different from the psychic one because it is timeless, it does not change; it is there from conception, it is there until death, it is there after death. Spiritual love is out of time and place and is one of the deepest—if not the deepest—of all the spiritual needs. Perhaps more than in most periods in history, it is the greatest spiritual need of the children of today.

The question now arises how the spiritual love, which has something that is free from the disturbances of the psyche, is to be kept alive. How is it not to be spoiled from the side of the parents and from that of the children? How are we to recognize it? One characteristic that I think eveyone can know is that it is nonpossessive. Whereas all psychic love has a certain possessiveness, a certain demand, the spiritual love has nothing of the kind. Another, about which I have already spoken, is that the dependence upon the changing condition of the psyche that dominates all psychic love does not apply to the spiritual love. It is the same always insofar as it is recognized. And the most important quality of spiritual love is that it always goes beyond the individual; it cannot be private or personal. Consequently, if spiritual love is established between parents and children, it will develop into the love of kind, the love of man. It will go further and develop into the love of God, or rather participation in the love with which God loves his creation. If the spiritual development of the child is to be assured, there must be satisfaction of these great needs. For that, there must be recognition by everyone concerned that there really are such needs. There must not be confusion as to what constitutes the spiritual need and what constitutes the other needs of our existence.

I have spoken very little tonight about spiritual needs in the religious sense, but it is, I think, obvious to everyone that religion is concerned with the spiritual nature of man. We make a great mistake if we subordinate the spiritual nature to the psychic or the organic nature: that is to say, if at any time we look upon religion merely as a useful part of man's life which serves to regulate and discipline the psyche or the social life of man. Whenever religion has been subordinated to social or psychic needs, it has lost its hold upon men; and in the end, religion itself has been blamed. If we look at history and understand these things even a little, we can see that it is those who have not understood anything about the spiritual life of man who have tried to understand religion in organic, psychic, or social terms only.

We may be sure that those who will speak to us about this will bring the religious significance of the spiritual problem before you in their different ways. I hope that, in making this introduction, I have not been guilty of suggesting answers or putting in front of you a picture of man and his needs which is biased by what happens to be my own belief and my own experience. If I have done that, then I will ask you to forgive me and simply to take what I have said as a contribution to the general discussion. If I have succeeded in being more or less impartial in presenting the problem, then what I have said can be of some value to those who will follow me.

QUESTIONS

Q. Do you think that the child's spiritual needs can be satisfied by parents who are spiritually hungry?

Mr. Bennett: I realize that in the way I have presented our problem, I may have given the impression that if only parents would set about it in the right way, they could do all that is necessary. I did say that families are on the whole not providing the spiritual environment, but I did not mean that this was because they were just too lazy or too careless—although this is sometimes true—but because they just do not know and have not got what is necessary to provide it. While not all parents can satisfy the spiritual needs of their children, there is very much that can be done not to spoil things that are now being spoiled. Even someone who is hungry can sometimes show another where to get bread.

Q. What is the connection between the word "ought" and what you said about duty? How can we know that we ought to do some duty?

Mr. Bennett: Some people hold that there is no such thing as a spiritual obligation. They say that there are only consequences. People who hold such a view would present to children the question of how they should or should not behave simply in terms of the consequences of behaving this way or that. They would say, "If you do this, you will be punished or you will spoil your future life, but if you do that, you will be rewarded." Put that way, there is really no "ought" about it. If there were no unpleasant consequences, then there is no reason why the act should not be done. Experience proves that this approach is not really effective. I would say that the word "ought" has a meaning not in relation to any results from it, but in the sense that there is an objective right, and that objective right causes obligations. Because there is an objective right, there is for all of us an obligation, irrespective of results, irrespective of whether it causes pleasure or pain. It is in this sense that I use the word "spiritual duty" as distinct from the teachings about right and wrong based upon the psyche of man. These are either theories of good and evil, or else pleasure-pain explanations of right and wrong actions. I believe that the sense of obligation is something very real in itself. I have always been impressed by Kant's development of this theme, and his conclusion that everything starts from what he calls the "categorical imperative." He asserts that there is one thing that everyone is sure of—much more than we are of the soul, or immortality, or God—and that is that we have obligation. I have that feeling myself; that everyone somehow, somewhere has the recognition that the obligation to do right does not depend upon reward and punishment, and that there is such a thing as objective right, or objective law, or Dharma, or the will of God, or whatever it may be called.

Q.   Do you really believe that the sense of obligation can be present in a child before it acquires awareness of self? And is the sense of obligation not something that must be acquired from others? Can you tell us what evidence there is of any spiritual awareness in young children?

Mr. Bennett: I cannot produce evidence, because this is a conviction that comes from my own observations; and if you do not agree, I cannot say that I must be right and you wrong. Nevertheless, I do believe that the spiritual nature is present in us from the very moment of conception.

Q.   I do not see how a young child can have any awareness of duty.

Mr. Bennett: It is not necessary to suppose that there is an awareness of duty; only awareness of a spiritual reality.

Q.   Surely a young child has nothing but instincts. Everything else comes from his contact with other people.

Mr. Bennett: I do not wish to be dogmatic. So let us leave it that we should not reject the idea that spiritual needs are just as real for young children as organic and psychic needs. It may be that this idea will help us to study the problem.

Q. Surely an obligation must be expressed and understood. We can recognize obligation in a commerical contract. Are not all obligations of the same kind?

Mr. Bennett: The contractual obligation is contractual. It depends upon the rewards of fulfillment and the penalties of failure. These may not be only financial. There are also rewards and penalties in the form of good and bad name, of honor and dishonor. But the spiritual obligation remains, even if no visible consequences are involved in the failure to fulfill it.

Q. Can you give an example of some spiritual quality or spiritual need that cannot be reduced to psychological terms?

Mr. Bennett: I have given the example of spiritual love. This is independent of the psychic state and therefore cannot be reduced to psychological terms.

Q. But you are using the same word. Surely love is love, and it can be understood without the distinctions you are trying to make.

Mr. Bennett: A hat is a hat. But you can distinguish between a top hat and a bowler hat, and sometimes it is very necessary to do so.

Q. But can you not give us at least one example where a word can only be used in what you mean by a "spiritual" sense?

Mr. Bennett: Yes, I would say that faith in God has no meaning except for our spiritual nature.

Q. I would like to mention something Dr. Steiner—who very much agreed with you about this obligation—said. He suggested that the way in which a child could become aware of obligations was to be personally attached to his mother for the first seven years. All the mothers in any community are doing many small things, like visiting their neighbors and taking in the other child when the mother is sick and doing a thousand little things. These are just the most important things for the small child to see for himself. Being attached to his mother, he would naturally go around and see that the mother was doing things out of a sense of obligation. By the time the child is seven and goes to school, he will have both a social sense and also the sense that the adult life is a fine life to grow up into. This, I feel, is very important for a child: that they must not think that the child life is something to hold onto, but that they are ending it in order to start life as adults.

Mr. Bennett: Yes, you bring something towards the solution of the problem; but also what you say does help to make clear what I really feel to be important about obligation. Spiritual obligation is more something that is experienced as a reality than something teachable. As soon as you try to teach this, you find you are teaching something else which probably touches only the psychic nature.

Q. I feel that parents are being allowed to shirk their duty. The parents should be responsible for the spiritual needs of the child up to seven years old. Nowadays they do not take this responsibility, they are even encouraged not to. Women are encouraged to go out to work, to hand their children over to others. The result of this is that at this particular period of life when the spiritual potential could be preserved, what is most necessary is taken away from them. If the parents would only recognize their duties, the child could then probably face the other kind of environmental influence with much less harm to his spiritual nature. I am convinced that this is a parent's task rather than one for nurses and teachers.

Q. I would like to add that we must consider the role of the state. To an increasing extent, state agencies are taking over responsibility for the care and education of children. Is there any way in which the spiritual needs of children can be satisfied when the state intervenes? It would be interesting to hear what the speakers have to say about these issues.

Mr. Bennett: I am sure that the speakers will take this into account. We know only too well that our present form of society is very unfavorable to the mother-child relationship being properly maintained. Mothers are being called away to other activities to an increasing extent in all industrial countries—and indeed, I am sorry to say, in all countries. Children, on the other hand, are being made the responsibility, at an early age, of people other than the parents. The question is: Is anyone able to suggest anything practical in front of this situation?

I feel that it is legitimate and interesting to ask, "Is there not at least something we can do?" because probably even doing a little could have very big results. It is not a question of saying, "Can we put back the clock?" That cannot be, no power on earth can do that. Can we perhaps persuade the whole human race that we are living very foolishly? That also is obviously impossible. But there is one thing that remains in the world, and maybe it is as strong as ever it was, and that is the love of parents for their children and the desire of parents to do what is best for their children. Therefore, our best hope is probably to help parents to understand the spiritual need of their children. If some contribution of a practical nature can be made during these talks, and if we can subsequently publish and disseminate these suggestions as widely as possible, who knows? Some good may be done.

Lecture 2

The Lord's Song in a Strange Land

Clifford John Williams

> *We sat down by the streams of Babylon and wept*
> *there, remembering Sion. Willow trees grew there,*
> *and on these we hung up our harps when the men*
> *who took us prisoner cried out for a song. We*
> *must make sport for our enemies; — A stave,*
> *there, from the music they sing at Sion! What,*
> *should we sing the Lord's Song in a strange land?*
> *Jerusalem, if I forget thee, perish the skill of my*
> *right hand! Let my tongue stick fast to the roof*
> *of my mouth if I cease to remember thee, if I love*
> *not Jerusalem dearer than heart's content.*

Psalm 137 gives the title and sets the theme that I shall
try to illuminate in the spirit of our overriding title,
"The Spiritual Hunger of the Modern Child."

It is a condition of our mortality that all our lives are
spent in "a strange land," strange in that by its very nature, it is different from the eternal values that together
make up "the Lord's Song." We live in the Babylonian
bondage of a physical body that, in common with all
other physical things, must grow, propagate, and die;
and which also has individual and peculiar beauties of its
own, as the Hanging Gardens of Babylon themselves

must have had. There are two vital necessities that we require in order to live in this strange land. We need to eat and we need to believe; in that order, it is true, but it is equally true that there is great misery and mischief where there is no belief. The varieties of belief are as numerous as the varieties of food and they can be taken raw or, in the hands of cunning cooks, can be served up in a great variety of ways. In the case of the first vital necessity, food, there is a growing tendency to leave the putting together of the ingredients to the cooking machines of the big manufacturers, to accept what it says on the packet or on the television commercial, to add water and pop into a moderate oven, and to be thankful that it is all so little bother, even if it costs those "few extra pennies" that the advertisers have persuaded us we can snobbishly afford. But, although new to food, the method has long been established and wonderfully successfully exploited in the field of belief.

Very early in human history, religion came to consist in the fulfillment of an ordered round of significant acts intended to promote fertility, ensure the well-being of the state, and protect the individual or the community from the anger of offended gods or the attacks of hostile evil spirits. How much easier and more comforting to put out a little food on a certain day at a certain time in front of a certain little idol, or great image, than to ask oneself what could be the real value of such things. Any tendency to question would be daunted by the grim examples made of those who would not worship the idols; punishments exacted in the name of a non-existent deity by fanatical upholders of the status quo. The majority accepted the diet of fear, sentimentality, or a mixture of the two together, with an occasional wondering to themselves why their spiritual hunger was, in many ways, not really satisfied.

When those exiles sat down beside the streams of Babylon, hung their harps on the willow trees and wept, they were not weeping for the real Jerusalem they had left behind. That had been almost as full of idols and idolatry as Babylon; its refusal to attend to the snatches of the Lord's Song it had heard had been one of the prime causes of its downfall. They wept remembering Sion, the idealized Jerusalem that was the great idea in the mind of the Jews, and they wept possibly more for their own betrayal of the idea of Sion than for their physical captivity. The thought, common to us all, of what might have been prevented their singing.

What was the "idea of Sion," and how had it come about? It had come about in the same way as every great development in the human experiment has come about; by a small number of individuals, usually "despised and rejected of men," who have not only heard the Lord's Song in this strange land—most of us do that at some time or another—but have dared to admit that they have heard it and to interpret it for their own generation. Such individuals have not been confined to one particular period or place, nor have they sprung from any one particular religion; but because of our terms of reference in Psalm 137, I would ask you to consider for a moment that unique line of men who were the Hebrew prophets. These particular singers of the Lord's Song are especially relevant for us today as they are the vital roots of the religion that so many nations profess to believe in today. It was these prophets who were mainly responsible for the great idea of Sion that the exiles wept over. They each brought a unique contribution as well as their general condemnation of idolatry: Amos with his insistence on righteousness, a right relationship between God and man; Hosea with, for his time and ours, the staggering idea of loving kindness and forgiveness; Isaiah with his insistence on the universality of God; and Jeremiah with perhaps the most significant message of all—that we are each one personally responsible for the growth and development of what we call our souls,

which brings to mind the later words of Socrates that
"the unexamined life is unlivable."

In his *Essays on Controversial Questions*, published in
1892, Professor T. H. Huxley wrote: "In the eighth
century B.C., in the heart of a world of idolatrous poly-
theists, the Hebrew prophets put forth a conception
of religion which appears to me to be as wonderful an
inspiration of genius as the art of Phidias or the science
of Aristotle. 'And what does the Lord require of thee,
but to do justly, and to love mercy, and to walk humbly
with thy God.' If any so-called religion takes away from
the great saying in the book of the Prophet Micah, I
think it wantonly mutilates; while if it adds thereto, I
think it obscures the perfect ideal of religion." To Professor Huxley's comment I would only add that men have
acknowledged the art of Phidias and the science of
Aristotle, but are being rather slower in accepting the
challenge of the Hebrew prophets. There is also the
further point that we accept the past achievements of
art and science and realize that they were only land-
marks on a road that we are still travelling, but people
are generally less willing to accept the fact that religion
is also continually developing and revealing new facets
of itself.

Of course, we are only babies. St. Theresa commented
that it is good to be reminded of the worthlessness of our
natures, if only in order to keep our humility. If you
prefer a contemporary comment, Professor Hyman Levy
has commented that if we made a "queue of mankind"
with one man representing a generation, it would be
three miles in length; about 15,000 generations. Three
paces back there was no theory of evolution, ten paces
back science was just beginning, one hundred paces back
and we are back before civilization. The fish and the
animals are our elders, and in many ways our betters,
upon which salutary note we come to the question of
the modern child.

"When we are born we cry that we are come to this great stage of fools," says Lear when madness has brought him to his senses. Then we cry for food, the first of those two necessities we mentioned earlier. Later we feel the need for belief. We have all of us been through these stages. Living where we do, for most of us the cry for food has been answered, and we manage to answer it for our children. We are proud of this; it is made much of at election time and our bonnie babies are featured in publications for the tourist trade, and sometimes even manage to oust the bikini girls off the front pages of the newspapers. "To do justly, and to love mercy, and to walk humbly with thy God." What about the first necessity, the need of food, for the large number of fellow human beings who are without it in a world that can well afford to provide it? There is even a danger now that our children are being overfed. I would ask you to reflect upon how far we are from realizing that we are our brother's brother, let alone asking Cain's question concerning whether we are our brother's keeper.

Our reaction to this question is vital to the child even before birth. Do we wonder to ourselves what he or she will do and have in the world, or what he or she will be in themselves? In *Don Quixote*, Cervantes tells us that there are only two families in the world, the Haves and the Have-Nots. If we are among the Haves, is our chief concern to preserve the time-honored, man-made walls that protect our little darlings from the Have-Nots, or to hope that the little darlings might set about knocking down the walls? If we are among the Have-Nots, is our chief concern to get little Nellie married into the Haves, or to give little Nellie some idea of how much she has anyway, simply by being a part of an experiment as fascinating and as unpredictable as the human experiment? The bad fairies, Fear and Ignorance, tend to dominate most christening parties and the sleeping beauties are dedicated to Mammon, that old sterile monster, one of whose other names is Respectability. This is no conscious human sacrifice, I hasten to add, and the ardent sincerity of most parents in being concerned about their children's well-being cannot be questioned; it is one of the oldest animal instincts. But the animals do not confuse the issue for their young. They pass on their skills, which will be passed on again, and follow the age-old round of the seasons with no guilt complexes, changing fashions, or self-imposed major catastrophes. They do not question that the race is to the strongest or that the weak must die. The rhythm of their days follows that of their antecedents through many centuries. The sounds they make have special meanings among themselves which outsiders cannot fathom. They accept the surroundings that they are born into and die unlamented at the end of their brief, pointless lives. But at least they have been consistent.

We set up idols in our public and private lives—one very prominent one at the moment is our old friend, Something for nothing, whether from a Bingo parlor or from the more luxurious setting of the new million-pound grandstand at the Ascot horseraces—idols which are all more or less complimentary to each other, except one rather small idol called "Gentle Jesus meek and mild," which is invoked from time to time officially, at times of national rejoicing or catastophes, or personally at marriages, funerals, and so on, and usually with such sentimental overtones that it is a good thing that we don't use it more often. This is the particular idol that a child sees us get rather solemn about—the others are much more fun—but which seems to contradict all the others. "I don't want you playing with those gypsy children"; "Do unto others as you would they should do unto thee." "You will understand when you are older"; "Except ye become as little children, ye can in no wise enter the Kingdom of Heaven." Children learn by imitation, and they will learn that we do not what we say they ought to do. But the little "ought to do," although watered down and distorted, is still powerful enough to linger and to confuse a young mind.

The provisions laid down in the 1944 Education Act made worship and religious training mandatory in all schools controlled by local authorities. These provisions regarding religious instruction are sometimes represented as a compromise arrangement, agreed to by the government in order that the religious bodies who once controlled the majority of schools might feel happier about the shift of authority. Probably there is something in this, and the government's prime concern was to get things settled rather than to assure religious educaton for future generations—a little offering to the little idol we have just mentioned, for respectability's sake. Consequently, we are faced with the situation that the divided loyalties of the world in general also confront the child at school. Schools so often, by public demand, are geared to place the major emphasis and tuition on those pupils who might get good examination results with the idea of a "well-paid job" to follow, or a job with "good status." This distorts the whole meaning of education, which should be primarily concerned with developing human potential for character, not for cash; for the cash can bring no real fulfillment, no real contribution to the human experiment, and certainly can do nothing to assuage the spiritual hunger of the modern child. Religious instruction, divinity, or whatever we may wish to call it, is the really important item on the school curriculum, the only all-embracing one. English, mathematics, history, and so on, are all departments of life— and very vital ones—whereas divinity involves the reason for life and the direction it takes. From it, if it is imaginatively and not sanctimoniously presented, we can best learn the one great remedy against spiritual hunger; namely, that what we get from life is entirely dependent upon what we put into it. If we make the prime aim of education the acquisition of a well-paid job, then all we are doing is offering sacrifices to another old sterile idol, Greed. Young minds are asking us for bread and we offer them stones which, whether precious or not, remain stones and can only be used effectively to build more Towers of Babel. This is not to imply that the vital links between all subjects and religious teaching should be emphasized or that the children should be always aware of them, but the connection should always be there in the teacher's mind.

The question will doubtless be asked, "Yes, but which kind of religion and what kind of teaching?" It was George Bernard Shaw who commented on the stupidity of people who say they never discuss religion or politics, since religion is the way we think and politics is the way we live. In other words, religion is concerned with ourselves in relation to the whole scheme of things of which we are a tiny part, while politics is concerned with ourselves in relation to our fellow-men. Thus, when I spoke of religious teaching, I meant the encouragement of that part of every individual that is always questioning and wondering about the purpose of our existence. We must not presume to assert that we have any final answers to such things; our business is to indicate that we are still groping for the way, and to pass on some of the results of earlier individuals who have wrestled with these things and have achieved varying degrees of success or failure. Once we set down an answer as final and declare that, "This is so," then we have set up an image; and because it is more comforting, for a while, to sit down in the shadow of such an image than to continue the journey, many will travel no further. The history of mankind, the whole of mental and physical evolution, in fact, is full of these Dead Ends where thousands have rested and turned their backs to the sun. The Lord's Song, the working out of the Divine Harmony, continues to develop, but it is difficult to hear in the "strange land" of Dead Ends, where the empty idols make so much noise. Like people who give nothing, these idols are always demanding sacrifice, and the toll they exact can be appalling. Child sacrifice is still with us in the name of Patriotism, Tradition, and Race Hatred, and society still attempts to keep attractive and symbolic those facades that sent those boys (I use that word in the literal, not its sentimental sense) to the slaughter on the Western Front in the 1914-1918 war.

There are, possibly, some ways in which the thousands who were killed on the Western Front in 1914-1918 might be envied by the disenchanted, rebellious youth today—the so-called "Teddy boys." Those young soldiers died, so many of them, believing in the cause that killed them, the image of the particular Dead End of the time; and death in such a mental state has compensations even for the young. Today the boys and girls can no longer be persuaded that there is any worthwhile substance behind all the facades. They have evolved that little bit further, so that they know when they are being bluffed, but that is as far as they can go. The result is a feeling of rejection without any resurrection or new revelation: They have not been taught how to look for such things. Their reaction is so sadly reminiscent of life in wartime London: a nervous frenzy in which the aim was immediate enjoyment, for who could tell how long the music would be able to go on playing? In any Post Office there are those comforting little charts, so clearly and beautifully presented, showing us that the largest item of government spending is devoted to armaments and kindred concerns, coyly named Defense; the kind of armaments that do not produce conquering heroes and are as lethal to "the girl he left behind him." This is not the place to discuss disarmament. I mention these things in order to ask how, in such an atmosphere, we can look for stability and spiritual nourishment for the young. These problems are mostly tackled outside educational establishments (which, as we saw, are obliged to turn out more candidates for the rat race), in the form of youth clubs, church clubs, the Y.M.C.A., the Y.W.C.A., the Youth Hostels Association, and so on. But while these institutions do admirable work with the finest intentions, it seems doubtful if they reach more than a small percentage of the adolescent population. This kind of "pastoral" approach may not be the one best calculated to attract the modern adolescent and may even be somewhat resented.

It is right that the young should rebel; that is really their main contribution to society. Through them we are constantly made to examine and face up to codes and habits that we come to accept all too readily. The young, as the old Chinese saying has it, are in the "house of tomorrow." We cannot enter into that house, and to throw stones at it is a sign of our jealousy, not our superiority. We set up more and more rules for young people and so often deny them the rights that we demand for ouselves in the pursuit of leisure and social intercourse. It is the adult attitude in a neighborhood that so often determines whether a gang is "delinquent" or just a "bunch of kids" seeking their vitally necessary social development—and social training, however inconvenient to society generally, is always formative and a natural development. The wish for personal emancipation is the right, the natural wish and is a sign of spiritual health, as is the wish to belong and to feel that somebody cares. Personal emancipation with parental support is what adolescents wish for and need, and it is this parental support that is often denied, even at the simplest level. The young remain with us at the cost of their own development and maturity and they must "use" or "misuse" their leisure in their own way. Skiffle groups and jazz cellars are not necessarily a misuse of leisure because they do not happen to fit in with our ideas of what a young person should be doing. What so-called "higher" use of leisure time have they been prepared for in school or by example from their elders?

Society would seem to be trying to prevent the misuse of adolescent leisure without first doing something about "the plank" in its own eye.

For a child the land is even more "strange" than it is for us. He grows up in a family and a house that he has not chosen and does not possess, and he is subjected to a series of rules and arrangements about which he is not consulted; he is indulged sometimes, carressed and played with, while at other times he is told to run along and not be a nuisance. He is injected, dosed, fed, and dressed according to the prevailing fashions in these things, and packed off to school to obey another set of rules and punishments about which he has not been consulted. He is told that some things are right and some things are wrong, but is rarely told why these things are so or whether they have been and will always be so.

It is a sign of the great strength in the life force, and a confirmation of the new hope that is born with each child, that despite all these things there comes a time when they turn around and ask some very, very pertinent questions. These questions are the sign of spiritual hunger which cannot be satisfied with smug and outdated cliches or references to "accepted standards." By their fruits these standards shall be known, and keen young appetites are quicker in reacting to the taste than our jaded ones. But these questions that the young disconcertingly ask us are also snatches of the Lord's Song in this strange land— a reminder of what we have forgotten.

The young have always sung the Lord's Song. The girl Antigone dared to ask Creon by what authority he decided who was and who was not fit for proper burial; Juliet rejected the immoral answer of "respectable" society to her problems; it is the girl Sonya, in Chekov's *Uncle Vanya*, who against all the boredom, despair, and muddle that chokes the life around her makes that marvelous affirmation of faith at the end of the play. I take the examples from the world's drama because in that we find the vital essence of life mirrored from age to age.

This spirit is not lacking in the young today. From infancy to adolescence they are still fired with the same
keen interest and the same dreams of what they wish to
do as they have always been—any parent or teacher
knows this in all its wonder and divine humor. But today
we do not give them the key of any door in their earlier
maturity, no pillar of cloud by day and pillar of fire by
night, but the possibility of a ghastly combination of
cloud and fire that will destroy them in the wilderness,
not lead them through it. They are not deceived by high
sounding phrases, and their awareness is well illustrated
in the references to their parents made by French adolescents. The general title that they have given them is "*les
croulants*," that is to say, "those who have begun to
collapse."

Where, then lies the remedy? How can we sing the
Lord's Song in a strange land? Are we to look for a sign,
something that will help us to combat the spiritual hunger of the modern child? "Jerusalem, if I forget thee,
perish the skill of my right hand! Let my tongue stick
fast to the roof of my mouth if I cease to remember thee,
if I love not Jerusalm dearer than heart's content." You
will remember that we said that this was no physically
real city that the exiles were remembering, but the "idea"
of a perfect dwelling place from which ignorance and
folly had taken them. This great idea had been built up
gradually by the prophets and great individuals from
early times, and is something that is still growing and
developing wherever it can. If the word God has no
meaning for you, call it the life force, evolution, the
human experiment, whatever you like as long as it gives
a direction and hope to human activity; as long as it
recognizes the potential in every human creature and
strives to bring that potential to fulfillment. Without
these incentives, the skill of our right hand will perish,
for we shall be using it for the wrong reason; for greed,
which never is satisfied and kills itself. Without these
incentives, our tongues will stick to the roof of our

mouth, for we shall say nothing that is creative or capable of development. Without these incentives, "heart's content" can only be an empty, meaningless, glib phrase. We shall never have anything but stones to offer to the spiritual hunger of the young unless we can demonstrate in a practical, everyday manner that *we* do justice, love mercy, and walk humbly. "For I desire mercy and not sacrifice": What an astoundingly simple and profound comment that was that came out of the world seven centuries before Jesus of Nazareth! Think of it applied to every facet of living. Think how often, in one form or another, publicly and privately, we settle for sacrifice rather than mercy, and how often we wish for mercy for ourselves. In the sphere that particularly concerns us—the relationship between parents and children—consider how many children have been and are sacrificed on the altar of parental ambition, parental selfishness, parental tyranny, and parental sentimentality; the very things that we deplore in the older and more primitive religions.

We each have to work out the notes of our own particular stave of the music they sing at Sion, and no one approach or method will resemble any other approach or method. The only thing that we can say with certainty is that unless we do work out our particular notes, there can be no easing of spiritual hunger or justification for existing. Such work is an end in itself. Success or failure is irrelevent, the acceptance of it is what matters. Mozart wrote music because that was his particular salvation; poverty and lack of recognition were only incidental, not fundamental things. The answer to spiritual hunger is not in some far off, "pie in the sky" dreamland, but in those things that are immediately to hand, the next notes on our stave. Only in this way are the songs of Sion composed, and the composer is—like the kingdom of heaven and, let us remember, the kingdom of hell—within ourselves.

QUESTIONS

Q. You mentioned that you feel the educational systems are not putting forward the right technique and the right principles. Have you any suggestions? It is all very well to say that we should enlighten the child in the spiritual life, but how?

Mr. Williams: I would like the personal approach of many teachers to be a little more practical, and of the headmasters and headmistresses to be a little more sympathetic to that particular department of education. So often it is the poor relation; it is not discussed at staff meetings and it is given to whoever is available to teach it. It often consists of writing out passages—not only from the Bible, but from other commentaries—and most of the words the children don't understand. This is probably good for their handwriting, but I don't think it is the point of religious education. But mainly, a more practical approach; that this is life. This is the basis from which we start; the practical point always. Incidentally, the Old Testament is much too much neglected in assemblies and everywhere else. It is so often Paul that is read. Children do not understand the involutions and convolutions of Pauline theology, they do not understand rabbinical discussions; they understand a practical point. They will discuss endlessly the man employing the laborers. The man who went out at 9 o'clock in the morning and said, "Right, you come work in the vineyard and you'll get a silver coin." And the same man goes out, last of all, at 5 o'clock in the evening and hires more laborers, and still gives them a silver coin. This is a practical point that might come up in trade union discussions. In fact, the dockers' trade union is close to that already. They say you must not victimize a man because he is waiting there for work; if the boats do not come in and there is not work, then he must be given a minimum. It is not fair to expect him to stand about and only pay him for the time that you can use him, because you have employed him. This is reasonable.

The crossing of the wilderness and the Ten Commandments can be looked at in the light of a military campaign in the Second World War: for example, Mountbatten arranging the Dieppe raid. You can't give the children the theological point, and I doubt if Moses gave the children of Isreal a theological point. Take the case of the graven images. What he wanted to point out was, "Yes, you have had marvelous images in Egypt, they have been marvelous, but it is not practical, we are going through the desert, we haven't got time to sit down and chip out one of your gods." It must be constantly emphasized that there is a time when you have got to sit down and think, "I am going to do this, and I shall have to proceed in this way, and if this is right for this man, why is it not equally right for this man, and if baby brother at home has all this food, why has baby brother in China only got half a bowl of rice, and why is that big truck by Lake Michigan tipping corn into the lake because they don't know where else to dispose of it?"

Q. A more social angle?

Mr. Williams: It is from this angle that I think it should be taught. Then it means something.

Q. You mentioned the point about sacrificing the child to various idols, and you said some of them were patriotism, war, and so on. Are you going to teach the child never to fight back, or are you going to teach them some self-defense?

Mr. Williams: Yes, the two things are rather different, they are not really on the same plane. The government committing the nation to war is not really on the same plane as the child meeting a nasty old man.

Q. Isn't it for self-defense?

Mr. Williams: This is of course an individual problem, but I think that if a child has been brought up in a healthy way, it should be possible for the child to have the attitude to cope with this kind of thing. A child should certainly be told of these kind of things, but it should always be emphasized that these people are sick, that they are not wicked. The small girl down the road had a rather unpleasant experience in the park the other day. She laughed, and it was the healthiest thing she could possibly have done because the man was completely disconcerted and went away. We have made so many barriers for ourselves, the children don't know how to break throught them. Even the business of birth is still not spoken about. It is getting a bit better now, but the husband is often still told, "It has nothing to do with you, your work is done, away you go"; no question of assisting with the delivery of the child.

Q. One still has to teach the child to defend himself, with judo for instance, at about ten years old?

Mr. Williams: Yes, I entirely agree. Just as he is taught to look both ways before crossing the road.

Q. The lecturer last week put before us the idea that there were three levels of hunger and three levels we could think about: physical, psychic, and spiritual. This evening we have spoken very much about the relationships between people rather than the relationship between people and spiritual things. Surely the hunger of a child is beyond the relationships between people. I am lucky to live in the country; after three hours in London today I was rattled to bits by my fellow men and women. Then I found a Roman Catholic church. I am not a Catholic, but never mind. The people in this church were finding something absolutely different. It seems to me that the children's hunger will stay until we can get further.

When my first child was put into my arms, I realized that it was not mine, but a being going right past me in the world. It was shown to me as forcibly as George Fox saw his things. It was the same with the other two children. If it were possible to get a large enough picture of this universe—no, of course we can't do that; of this earth—then we could see we are receiving a great stream of souls through the mother and father. Surely the religious upbringing should be to say "Man has reached this stage in his understanding of God." Surely it was just one of God's extra divine wangles when he sent a Buddha or a Christ. A nine year old wants to hear living stories of the heroes, it is part of the living food of the spiritual part of the child. It is this larger vision fostered by the Quakers in their silence and the Roman Catholics in the church this evening which can give the necessary riches to children.

Mr. Williams: I am sure that was Jesus' point; that the kingdom of heaven lies within you, and also that when you pray you enter into a chamber by yourself and in the silence there find an answer. The difficulty with children is that one has got to somehow try to foster this and to get them to find these resources within themselves against the opposing camp which is, as it were, shouting the opposite thing to them. This is the thing that is difficult to preserve in the child, this capacity which they have when they are small of complete absorption and wonderment.

Q. I also wondered if there is any attempt by the authorities to teach something about other religions without belittling them. Should we not learn to understand each other's religions a little more?

Mr. Williams: Yes, I think it is appalling that there should be such insularity. I always try to give some time to other convictions and beliefs in the classes I teach. The children are always very interested in such things as the five-fold path of Buddhism. They often say, "Aren't they all alike?" which is true of course. They see the relationship between them, and also how they are adapted to the different climates and peoples. I am afraid that most of the literature that is given to teachers is inadequate.

Q. Can we do anything about the way in which teachers are trained?

Mr. Williams: One has to remember that in the training college they are so often concentrating on the further development of the potential in each student. What is always emphasized, and rightfully so, is that you cannot be taught how to teach, but the more you know yourself, the better you will teach. The training courses do attempt to develop the personality of the student. It would be an immense help to learn Hebrew in preparation for teaching divinity. I think the children should be introduced to the Bible by a history of the Bible itself. It should be explained that here are sixty-six different books all put into one; that they have all come from different kinds of people—shepherds, kings, priests; and that this is as far as they got, how they expressed themselves, how they felt, which has now all come together. The seed is planted within the children that they are part of a tremendous tradition of seeking and striving after some sort of spiritual fulfillment; they fit into this and without it they would not be complete.

Q. I understand the educational authorities don't insist that the teacher should belong to any religious persuasion whatsoever. But he may have to teach religion?

Mr. Williams: Religion is one of those subjects you don't have to teach. This is why there is difficulty in finding people to teach it who are really interested in it. It is usually the person who will oblige, or the vicar's wife who comes up twice a week.

Q. What do you think of George Bernard Shaw, who tells us that a child should be able to express his own nature?

Mr. Williams: Yes, insofar as it is possible, I do agree. Shaw also made the point that the vilest abortionist is he who attempts to mold the child's mind, simply because the only mind that we can mold—and even that not very adequately—is our own. So that all the things that we can pass on to our children seem to be the prosaic things: We can definitely tell them to look left and right when they cross the road, and that to eat this is better than to eat that. We can give them definite answers on things like this. I think it is dangerous, and I think we immediately set up an image if we say that, "This is it," or "God is like this," or "Do this because God says so." Those sentimental colored pictures of Jesus take such a lot of removing from minds that have been subjected to them. Mark is a marvelous place to start. We get a picture of the tremendous practicality of Jesus, the compelling power of his look, that he was from Galilee, that he had an accent, that he had black, probably rather greasy hair and rather a large nose. This is very embarrassing to many people. This is the picture one has to give even more forcibly to counterbalance the molding that has gone on before.

Q. Am I right in thinking that the trouble with children is that they are not interested in God and hearing about God? I was taken to Quaker meetings in Edinburgh as a child, and I don't remember a thing about them, but I remember the smiles on the people's faces, and I came to think of them as good people. So I remembered them.

Mr. Williams: That is what I mean, because as soon as you say "God," you put up an image. One cannot define these things, and the child, up to a certain age, is unconsciously or intuitively aware that he is part of all this. He feels an immediate relationship with objects, and if you start introducing certain ideas of God and this kind of thing, you are in danger of shattering that immediate communion that children have with life as a whole.

Q. How then will you do it?

Mr. Williams: You can introduce it when they ask something specific about flowers, or how something is made. You can then begin to introduce the idea that they are part of an enormous pattern. It should always be at the back of your mind to convey that they are part, as you are part, of an enormous, marvelous scheme, a wonderful adventure. This sense of imagination and wonder is what we must preserve in them. It is when we rob them of that that we betray them. Each individual case presents a different problem. It is a shame, in many ways, that things were written down, because I am sure that Jesus and the prophets went out every day and dealt with the particular problem at hand. They did not have some great thing such as, "Next Tuesday week it is going to be marvelous," it was the immediate thing that came to hand with which they dealt. But as soon as you write it down, as soon as you start putting things around it, it becomes dead like a stone instead of something living and vital, as children are everyday.

Q. "What happens when we die?" This seems to me to be the epitome of the connection children want with what you say, and with the actual happenings of life.

Q. It is a great comfort for the children when grown-ups say, "I don't know."

Q. You can know that mistakes are being made in every generation. I don't want to introduce things to my children that are introduced to other children. They should not be given means of expressing themselves in a bad way: guns and so on. It is not right for any parent to accept that their child should be treating his friend as a cowboy or Indian. I want to prevent it for my children. If it does happen, I shall try to get over it, get it out of their system.

Mr. Williams: It has arisen, or course, because of this idol we have set up, that man is somehow associated with banging and bashing. It is very difficult to combat it, especially when the child has to go to school. It is wrongly channeled, of course. When a boy tears a butterfly to bits, I don't think it is primarily cruelty. I think it is primarily curiosity: "How was this put together?" They must have a physical outlet, but it is not given the right direction. There should be much more drama in schools, which is physical and imaginative. They are much calmer after it.

Q. All scripture teaching must be wrong to some extent; parents and teachers must live by what they believe.

Mr. Williams: As far as small children are concerned, these things are never conveyed in words, but in atmosphere. One has to talk to them in words, but "It is not what you say, but the way you say it," as Miss Mae West so rightly said. The child needs to feel he is consulted, that things are explained, that he can come and ask you any question under the sun and receive the most honest answer you are able to give—not confusing him by taking it wider than the question that he has asked, but speaking about the immediate thing on his mind. He can accept it and go away and absorb it. Children need to live in an atmosphere in which they know it will be all right to go home and ask, and to know they won't be told, "Oh, we don't talk about that."

Lecture 3

Dr. Maria Montessori and the Child

Dr. Mario Montessori

I hope you are not going to be disillusioned by what I say. There is a shining figure associated with the name of Maria Montessori, who revolutionized the whole world by her love, by her science, and by her spirituality. When I dare to come with her name in front of the public, I feel very jittery, I assure you. But I'll try to do my best.

I must begin by saying, since this program is called "The Spiritual Hunger of the Modern Child," that I don't believe that the child has a spiritual hunger. The child certainly does express a physical hunger, and even more greatly expresses a psychic hunger, but spiritual hunger it does not express. And it does not express it, I am persuaded, for the simple reason that the child is the essence of spirituality, and being the essence of spirituality, it does not express spiritual hunger. For instance, wine gives a little bit of a better feeling when one is depressed, and one may feel the need of that solace for strength when depressed. But the wine itself does not feel the need for wine. This is the case of the child. It is very difficult to express. I do not get it across in one-year courses. Neither, I think, will I get it across tonight in one hour. The only way I can hope to express something of it is to describe the impact that the spirituality of the child had on the dramatic life of Dr. Montessori.

Dr. Montessori was an extraordinary person; she was very strong-willed, or she never would have become a doctor. You cannot imagine the difficulties in the family and in the public opinion that she had to overcome in order to study medicine. At that time, a woman who went among men, and especially among naked bodies which she cut to pieces, was not considered a "nice" person. During her studies she was ostracized, and when she succeeded in becoming a doctor, it was a great achievement, a great triumph. People then began to realize her value. She was brilliant in her lectures and she had a good sense of justice. She threw herself into the fight for feminism, which was then starting, and for socialism. She went from nation to nation and gained a brilliant reputation.

Dr. Montessori had done some work with institutionalized mentally retarded children as well, with so much success that when they entered the public state examinations they were able to pass the examinations at the same level as the normal candidates. This gave her a certain suspicion that not everything was completely right with the educational systems of the time. She went to study in France, Germany, and England, and found the pupils — as she described them in her book, *The Discovery of the Child*, "like butterflies fixed by a pin to a board," reduced to immobility because obedience and silence were essential. She felt, "this is not discipline, this is annihilation of the human being." And that was la Montessori.

She had a brilliant career in front of her. She was a young woman doctor in Italy, she was a lecturer at the University of Rome, she had done this occasional work with mentally retarded children, and everybody expected her to have a very successful future in her field. She was expecting this, too, until she received the impact of the spirituality of the child and left everything to follow it.

What were the characteristics of the child at the time? According to both the psychologists and the ordinary people, the child was an irresponsible person. Children could not concentrate; they passed from one thing to another and always depended on others. When their mothers asked them to do something they would say, "No, I don't want to do it; you do it for me." If in school they were made to work, it was very difficult; indeed, they had a lot of mental fatigue. One could not even trust them very much with sweets; if you left them with a box of chocolates within their reach, well, the whole of the chocolates disappeared, and the following day they had a tummy ache, perhaps, or something like that. Then, they always wanted new toys, but when they had them, they played with them for a little while and then got tired and dropped the toys, and they left them there, and then the mother had to run after them and tidy up. As far as cleanliness was concerned, in Italy the mothers sometimes had to go after their children without them noticing and had to scrub them and clean them, because as soon as they saw the mother coming they began to run away, knowing that she was going to scrub them. So they were dirty, they were disorderly, they lacked concentration, they were gluttons, they stole sweets, and everything breakable had to be put out of their reach because they would go to it, drop it, and break it. Such was the child, and thus it was described by official psychology.

So, there was Dr. Montessori and there were the children; but she had never had experience with normal children and the opportunity came by chance in 1907. Some new tenement buildings were being put at the disposal of poor people within a housing scheme, and in this group there were about thirty or forty families,

with about fifty children, including some very young
ones from three to six. The parents had to go out and
catch some casual job during the day — carrying a bag,
or carrying something from the street up to a flat, or
washing a horse, or anything like that in order to get
some money. But the children, what could be done with
the children when they were left alone? They were left
completely alone and they were little savages. They could
entertain themselves, but how? By playing about, but
playing about meant that the building was being spoiled,
that the stairs were made dirty, that all sorts of damage
was being done. So this newly established society said,
"We have to do something about the children. What can
we do? Let's collect them together, and let's give them
to this marvelous lady who knows all about health;
she is a woman doctor, she is very clever." They asked
her if she would take care of them. Dr. Montessori accepted the care of these children, and a room and lots
of toys were put at her disposal.

So this was the situation: On the first day there was
a little group of savages. Their noses were running, and
as soon as they saw a stranger, they ran away. They were
afraid of anybody who approached them, so you can
imagine what happened when they were all in one room
on the inauguration day. All the children were howling,
and in order to make them stand somehow near one another, each child was asked to grab the pinafore of the
child in front. Here they were, these fifty children,
coming inside and crying, with a group of people around
the platform, nice ladies dressed up with beautiful hats
with feathers and things like that.

Another aspect of the situation, of course, was that
these children had absolutely no religion. The parents
were people who had very little to do with religion;
many had quite recent prison-terms behind them, and
they had no time for churches and things of that kind —
my goodness, no. Dr. Montessori herself was not particu-

larly spiritual. On the contrary, at that time science was against religion on the grounds that you cannot prove God's existence, so it must all be nonsense. Dr. Montessori was then a positivist.

So we start with this group of children, belonging to that group of parents, and a positivist. The positivist was a scientist, so the first thing she did was to make psychological experiments. Her aim was to see if the use of the apparatuses with which she had so much success in the education of mentally retarded children could serve as a sort of mental hygiene for these children, to make their minds sounder and straighter. These apparatuses were learning games that the children could manipulate themselves. In this non-verbal way, the children were presented with basic concepts about the material world — such as number, rough and smooth, shape, sound, size — through their own tactile experience, without direct dependence on an adult. She saw, to her great surprise, that while with the mentally retarded children she had to strive very hard in order to gain their interest, these little ones became intensely interested. They began to work with the apparatuses, and after they had finished they began all over again. She saw concentration so strong in these small children that she could not believe it. She had studied and knew that official psychologists had said that the children were incapable of concentrating — and these children were concentrating.

Another point was that although there were a great many toys, these children did not play with them. One day she said, "They probably don't know what to do with them," and gathered a group of children and started to show them. They had a kitchen and they had a doll who had a kitchen, with little plates and other things, and she showed the children how to play with these things. The children were very interested for a little while, and then they went back to their previous occupations. Another strange thing was that they liked to do housework — menial work such as scrubbing the floor and washing the tables — instead of playing with the beautiful toys. They preferred work to play, and there was concentration.

Dr. Montessori also noticed that every time the teacher put away the material with which they worked, the children went after her. The teacher said, "Go and sit down," but the children still went after her. "You know," said the teacher, "these children are disobedient." But Dr. Montessori had an idea: "Perhaps they want to do it themselves," she said, "Let us see what happens." And that was it. They wanted to see where everything went, and to know where each piece was, and they wanted to put it there themselves. From that there began to develop love for other things also, and anything that was out of place, they put into place. This was in complete opposition to what was happening in ordinary life: There the children were disorderly, always leaving things lying around, and the mother had to run after them.

Many things happened now. One was the growth of silence. These children had been completely unruly, so much so that when they were coming out of school their lives were in real danger, for they ran and bumped into everything, throwing each other down and shrieking madly. People said, "School is out now — we can hear the children." At home children would often play at who could shriek louder. Silence scared them to death. But now, these children preferred silence; they began to move around on tiptoes.

Another observation Dr. Montessori made was that when a child who was having difficulties with what he was doing was offered help, he would refuse and say, "I want to do it myself." Previously, the children had always been saying, "Mama, you do it for me, Mama, you do it for me." Another extraordinary fact: After they had finished working, instead of being tired, they were more rested, quieter, healthier, and happier. That was also completely opposite to what happened elsewhere: The child should not work except for a short while because there was the problem of mental fatigue. I must mention one last surprise. Dr. Montessori had given the children the letters of the alphabet and told them the phonetic sound of the letters. The letters were cut out in sandpaper and pasted on little squares of cardboard. One day, a four and a half year old began to write, and he was so surprised himself that he shouted to the other children, "I can write, I am writing." All the other children went around to look at this child writing, and then they said, "Me, too," and grabbed pieces of chalk and began to write with enormous enthusiasm. They wrote everywhere, on the wall, on the floor, everywhere. These were children of four years and a half. To teach children to write was the torture of the elementary school. I remember my own case. We had special pens, and there was a teacher, and if this finger was held like that, she had a cane and whack! from behind on the finger. And these children discovered writing spontaneously.

Other unexpected phenomena took place, and Dr. Montessori was unable to account for them. The only thing she had done was to give them freedom, freedom to choose their tasks, and she had shown them the technique of using each object. That was all. There was no directive from the teacher; each child did as he chose — one went to wash the table, one went to take on one of the apparatuses, another one went to shine shoes — each one was completely busy and happy.

What impressed Dr. Montessori most was the spirituality of the child. They were completely independent as far as their own work was concerned, but if anything disruptive happened — for instance, if something was spilled, or the teacher knocked something down with her apron — the children immediately went to help and to put it right. They did not fight anymore, there was no snatching of objects from one another. A perfect sort of communism reigned. Communism is a dirty word nowadays, but it isn't with children. They had the use of all the objects, but nobody possessed them; they loved the objects, and took care with them, and had respect for the work of the other children and for the children themselves. They began to feel intuitively when people were suffering. One time a lady came, dressed in black. She had lost her husband and she came there just to sit down. A little child went to her, took her hand and patted it and went away. Nobody had told the child anything.

Thus Dr. Montessori saw these souls becoming alive, shedding their possessiveness, shedding their coarseness. I am going to read a few words from her book called *The Secret of Childhood* to show you her feelings: "It took time for me to convince myself that this was not an illusion; after each new experience, proving such a truth, I said to myself: 'I won't believe yet, I will believe it the next time' and thus, for a long time, I remained incredulous, and at the same time, deeply stirred." What Dr. Montessori had seen was the renunciation of all that was considered sin, and the emergence of the spirit through the influence of no one, but only by the possibility of the children working and expressing themselves. This community of little beings of three to six who had spontaneously made a perfect society touched this woman. And this positivist, who disbelieved in religion, continues: "One day, in great emotion, I took my heart in my two hands, as though to encourage it to raise to the heights of faith, and I stood respectfully before the children, saying to myself: 'Who are you then? Have I perhaps met with the children who were held in Christ's arms and to whom divine words were spoken? I will follow you to enter with you into the Kingdom of Heaven.' "

The children have made a great convert: Dr. Montessori, a scientist, a disbeliever. And she did, she followed Him. She left her career, she left her brilliant position among the socialists and among the feminists, she left the university, she left even the family and followed Him. She was not the only one impressed. As soon as this phenomenon became known, the press came, because the press is always there when there is something new. Newspapers began to talk about it, and the school became a center of pilgrimage. People came, crossing the oceans, crossing the continents, to see the "discovery of the human soul," as they said. There were Hindus, Buddhists, and Christians, princes and ambassadors. From all the world these people came. It made such an impact that by 1912 the Communist party, at a congress in Geneva, declared it one of the human rights to be educated by the Montessori method, while Christian people were speaking with praise about the "converted children" because it looked as though they had become converted.

But who converted them? What converted them? If to you the term "conversion" means that these children had assumed the behavior of people who are considered spiritual, then it means that spirituality is ingrained in the human being. Nobody talked of spirituality; it arose spontaneously. Certainly Dr. Montessori had not converted them, and who else? The walls of their room? So if it arose, it means that it was inside. This brings us back to what I was saying before: I don't believe that children have a spiritual hunger, I believe that they are the spiritual essence. In this there is a hope for our days, because the problem arising from the neglect of children going out to work has become universal.

Why were those fifty children — to whom the word "converted" was applied — different from other children? Or rather, why were other children different from these fifty children who were termed converted? Evidently there was something lacking, and that something was the possibility of developing their spirituality. They lived in conditions in which this spirituality could not express itself, and their behavior was the rebellion of the spirit which showed itself in many ways, such as gluttony, violence, the desire for attention, and total disregard for all others. According to the statistics, there has never been such an increase in delinquency, such an increase in mental disequilibrium, as there is today. But if physical and psychic hunger are satisfied, then there must be something lacking, and it is this: the possibility for the life, which is the spirit, to be able to feed itself.

Spirituality, being an essence, is not felt. A child feels physical and psychic hunger, but spiritual hunger in a child is not felt because it is unconscious, and therefore we give no importance to it. If we applied the same thing to the body, we would only be appreciative of what in our bodily functions reaches our consciousness. I don't feel the liver working, nor the kidneys, I don't feel the blood rushing inside my veins; yet they all have a function. When something goes wrong, then we become conscious of it. It is the same with spirituality: you do not feel it, but it has a function, and you feel it when there is something wrong, as there is today. What happens if you pay no attention to the symptoms of these non-felt organs? If you pay no attention to them, your body dies, and that is what we are in danger of today: society is in danger of dying. We have the danger of destruction over our head like the sword of Damocles. But in the child there is hope.

That is why Dr. Montessori left everything to follow the child. But following the child does not imply that the child is going to tell us what to do. It means that we have to recognize that there are certain characteristics in the child which may help us to help him. And if we must serve the child, as Dr. Montessori suggests, this does not mean that we consider the child superior to us in reason, in the wisdom given by experience, or that we become dependent on him and do what he says. Rather, we must realize that there is in him a part of divine creation which is at a loss in this difficult world, in which even we grown-ups cannot keep straight. How can that poor, little, unconscious feeling of the child keep its equilibrium and steer its way in this maelstrom of today, unless we serve this divine part in the spirit.

We give far too much attention to the conscious, and hardly any to the unconscious. And yet, it is the unconscious which directs everything in the life of the child, from birth and even from before birth. Take this example, for instance. I always give it because, as you know, you may have difficulties in understanding me. I speak English since many years, but my English is not English, my pronunciation is not an English pronunciation, not an American, it is a sort of mixture of this and that. And yet, as you see, I even have the courage to go out and talk in public. I have studied grammer, I have teachers, and I have dictionaries. I have all the possible help, and yet, my English is not English. You go to Greece, every blessed child speaks good English. Who taught them? Where were the professors, the books, the teachers? And yet each one of us speaks best his own mother tongue. It is not the mother tongue, it is the child's tongue. You realize the fact that the child does not go consciously to study, and yet he gets every inflection of pronunciation. He takes the formation, the grammer, at a period when he has no intelligence, no organized intelligence, because the learning starts at birth. What intelligence have you got at birth? No conscious intelligence. It is not the will of the child; there is something inside the child, another intelligence guiding him, which gives him parts of its divine powers.

There are other aspects to this unconscious learning.

The first lesson the child gives us is love. He has love in himself, and he knows how to arouse love in others. When you go out of your country, after a while you begin to feel homesick, no matter where you came from. If you come from the desert, you say, Oh, yes, this nice city, beautiful city," but after a while you begin to say, "Oh la la, so much noise, so much confusion, give me peace in my desert, there I feel God, there I feel..." If you come from the mountains you hate the plains, and if you come from the plains, you hate the mountains. And if you come from Italy you like spaghetti and you do not like English food, and if you come from India you like rice and curry and never other things. What has made us this way? Our consciousness? Did we go to study the different kinds of cooking and say, "I prefer this, I prefer that?" No, it is something unconscious that we have absorbed and which gives us the directive. That is the unconscious of the child.

Spirituality cannot be taught. Spirituality is there, but to keep it, just as to keep the body, you must feed it from birth. People nowadays discuss whether the first Italian children that Dr. Montessori worked with showed those marvelous results because it was something Italian, or because they were in a Catholic country, so it can be ascribed to the Catholic religion. But it happens in India, it happens in Africa, it happens in many countries where nobody teaches them anything. All children show the same characteristics and the same conversion that I described in detail earlier. I take this to mean that the essence of the human being is like that — no matter what surroundings, no matter what civilization, no matter what religion. But there is the question of life. One has to live, one has to give to the subconscious the chance of organizing itself into a morality, into a sense of obligation. In this the mothers are very helpful, but it is not in the hands of the mothers alone; there is still the child himself.

Two people get married — normal people who are quite

selfish, who try to get as much fun as they can, to dress as nicely as they can, to amuse themselves as much as they possibly can — and then something happens. A stranger comes, because a child is a stranger, they never knew him before he was born. There we are, we have to clean him because he is dirty, we have to feed him, we have to stay up at night sometimes, if he cries we hug him and we caress him, we begin to put aside money and say, "I must not buy this because this little creature will need it later on." What bigger conversion is there than this? Do you suppose that a preacher, no matter how inspired, could have persuaded these two young people: "There is a paralytic person who cannot feed himself, he gets all dirty, you must stay up all night with him and clean him and take care of him and enjoy it"? No. There it is; this love has been aroused by what? By a few pounds of flesh which did not exist before. There is the power of the child. When you see the child himself, he is all power. How does it come that there is such a powerful abstract love, so much bigger than the child himself?

I was speaking before about language and home-sickness. A child also experiences something like this. No matter what the group is, it is united by religion, customs, habits, food, and so forth. You can see Indians coming together here and eating the nice English food, and saying, "Oh, that nice curried rice, how much we miss it." They meet because they have the same customs, and understand one another. The same holds true for Italians and all other groups. There is a community of feelings, of customs, of habits, and of understanding. What does the child do about it? I have seen little girls four years of age ask, "Mother, when are you going to prick my ears so that I can put my earrings like you have them?" And later on, "Mother, when am I going to put on this corsage that you have?" In Italy these are often made with velvet, rather ornate, and very much a part of a woman's dress. The child says in effect, "I want to be like you, I want to become like you. I don't judge whether you are an aristocrat, whether you are white, green, or yellow, whether you are a cannibal or a vegetarian. I want to be like you." Isn't that very much like that charity described by St. Paul when he wrote to the Corinthians, "Charity doesn't judge, doesn't condemn, has enormous patience, accepts everything '? Isn't that the child, the young consciousness of the child? Can you have more spiritual love than that? And we have it in front of us everyday.

God took precautions when he created the mother and child. He attached the child to the mother; not only by love, but by the fact that the child's first food comes from the mother, so the child goes with the mother. The mother cannot leave him at home, and so when she goes to church and has a child only one month old, the baby comes with his mother. For Spirituality and for moral obligations, it is the same process of unconscious learning as it is for language. It is the unconscious of the child that takes it in. But if the child is isolated from language, do you suppose that he could learn language? He would not. The child goes into society, he grabs from society, and he grabs you, not what you teach him. You and your expressions, your behavior; how much do you imagine the child doesn't know because he is not conscious of it? The consciousness of the child may not know, but his subconscious does.

To conclude my talk, I would like to tell you two stories from my own experience. In India one day, I saw a teacher and a child. The teacher was looking very intently at the child who was doing something which seemed to me completely useless and dirty. She was scratching the ground with her finger and I went to see more closely. There was an ant which on one side had only one leg left and on the other side two legs broken and it was struggling on in this condition. This little child was smoothing the way for this ant. In India, there is respect for life; this child of two years and a half was already filled with this respect for life. Obligations and religious feelings come into sight if we have the chance to observe them. Another child, also in India, came to our school when he was about three years old, and had never seen an elephant in procession. He often asked, "When is the elephant procession? When is the elephant procession?" One day at last it came. I called him, "Elephant procession. Come." He was working with some beads, he ran down to see it, but when I followed a little later, he was not there. I wondered where he was, since he had wanted to see it so much, and I went back to the class. There he was, crying, picking up his beads one after another. "But what are you doing here?" I said, "there is an elephant procession." And he answered, "Yes, but I have to put these things back." Then I asked him, "But who told you to put them back?" His reply was, "I told me." He had been accustomed to the fact that if something was spilled one had to pick it up. Imagine the conflict in that child. Whether we realize it or not, the subconscious of the child is a much more powerful agent for good, beauty, and religion than any conscious teaching later on. You cannot impart spirituality to seven year olds by teaching moral precepts.

I could tell you many more things about children but I will say only this: All around us hope is continually renewed. Children are being born everyday; they are like a rain of souls that God sends us in order to help us on our way towards the future. He is with us, but we do not know Him and do not consider Him. I would like to finish with one indication that Dr. Montessori gives to a teacher — not as a prayer so much, but as a reminder — to guide them in their behavior and in their attitude towards children. It may well serve us, and other people who are not teachers: "Help us, oh God, to enter into the psyche of childhood, so that we may know, love, and serve this child in accordance with the laws of Thy justice, and follow Thy holy Will."

QUESTIONS

Q.   Could you clarify what you said about using the consciousness too much?

Mr. Montessori: We go to an individual who is already quite formed, and when we want to transmit something, we do it through consciousness and therefore we use reason. We do not give enough importance to the experiences that the child has, which he absorbs subconsciously. It is something like language: Certainly the child does not realize that he studies a language, it is something which he learns subconsciously. But then one day this process in him stops. Suppose that we have to teach language by lessons — that is not the same thing. This is confirmed by our own experience during the whole of history; first the things were done, and then they were discovered. They were there all the time, but at one point you became conscious of them. Now, if there was nothing there, of what can you become conscious? The same holds true for this spiritual exchange that takes place between the child and society. If the child has no opportunity of getting anything from society — then he has nothing to become conscious of; and if you try to make him conscious of it later on, when the time for it is past, you'll find it extremely difficult. Dr. Montessori describes sensitive periods in the child's development: There are certain psychic powers present at one age which change at the next. Through these psychic powers, what is acquired at one age remains to be made use of at a later age. But if nothing has been acquired, the child will face difficulties later. We have read a few examples in history of savage children found in forests; it was extremely difficult for them to adapt to civilized life or to understand morality.

Q.   I have experienced with my own child, aged two, almost everything Mr. Montessori stated: He prefers work to play, he can love other beings, help them, and give away his toys. There is one thing that worries me though. He used to give his toys to other children, until one child started taking them away from him and knocking him down. Since then he has started hanging on to his toys. Is there something you could say that would help here?

Mr. Montessori: I think if you sent him to a Montessori school he would be better. Not because of Montessori, but because there he will have an opportunity for more types of occupations, and meet other children who also exchange things, and little by little this attitude he has learned would disappear. I know that at that age impressions such as those you describe are very powerful, but a society of children has very often been found to be a cure for a great many disorders. Yours is not a disorder at all, it is a very natural thing that will disappear by itself even if you don't send your child to a Montessori school.

Q. Should that child be kept away from the more aggressive children or should he be encouraged to rough it out?

Mr. Montessori: Rough it out with them.

Q. How do you recover the child? In the turmoil of the world, all kinds of influences act on the child. How are we to restore the balance? The child is the essence of spirituality, as you said. But some grown-ups seem to have lost it. How can the essence of spirituality be maintained throughout life?

Mr. Montessori: How do you maintain yourself throughout life? How do you maintain yourself physically? Spirituality is life. You may recover spirituality because you never lost it, and people who thus recover it are called converts. But according to Dr. Montessori, there is naturally a whole system to help maintain spirituality. What matters is always to help the child through its different psychic phases. For instance, if God did not exist, he should be invented for the child. Especially when the child is young, he needs the assurance of something stable, something which is right. That is why I said you cannot teach morality by words, you cannot teach obligation by words.

I will give you an example: A mother was telling her child how terrible it was to lie. The child was impressed. Then one day he heard his mother answering the phone. She was on the point of going out to a tea; and on the phone was an old aunt who wanted to come, one of these awful old aunts, you know, that came at the most inopportune moments. The mother suffered from migraine headaches, and when she had a migraine she was horrid, and the aunt knew it. So this lady, who was all dressed up to go out, said, "Oh dear auntie, oh no, today no, it is not convenient. I have such a terrible headache and I know that you would not like it." And the aunt knew that she would not like it, so she said she would come another day. The child was there, and the child began to weep, and the mother did not understand: "Why do you cry?" "You have lied, you have no migraine, you only want to do tea." The mother was shocked, she had never thought about that. We teach the children not to lie, but we lie, almost every day, one time or another. We give the children the impression that we ourselves do not do what we ask them to do.

But you can explain this to children: "No human being is perfect, there is only one entity that is perfect, and that is God. In God, you can have faith and trust." Children accept that readily, because it corresponds to something inside them, and it is a great consolation for the child to know that there is an entity made of love, love eternal, looking after everyone, also looking after him. And very often this sense or feeling of protection and this feeling of perfection helps the children to understand their mothers better. She says, "God is good, he will forgive you." The child understands also the faults of the father, and understands his own faults. We have to show our children that while we are striving as much as we possibly can, we are certainly not perfect. This is already a consolation and shows him that there is something stable.

At different ages, this need the children have for moral stability shows in different ways. Small children, up to three years and a half or four, have a special need for protection. I remember a prayer that a mother was teaching her child, and the child always asked for it at night when she went to bed. She would say, "Mama, let us say the prayer," and Mama would say, "Oh God, keep us in the night, keep Papa safe, Mama safe, and the little girl safe." The first time she said the prayer, the little girl added, "And keep safe John (who was the servant) and Mary (who was the cook) and the cat and the dog." The love of the child is a little bit like universal love. In this way, you can support the child during this stage. At seven or eight, the children's needs are different. They are beginning to feel the need of distinguishing what is good and what is bad, to be quite sure about it. After they have made this distinction, they feel the need of learning. Then you can teach them the Commandments, religion, and things like that. And after that, they begin to feel the need of becoming soldiers of Christ.

Puberty brings yet another stage. There were children, for instance, in one of our schools in France, who suddenly decided to adopt some old people who had nobody; they lived, they had enough to eat, but nobody kept them any company. So the children took turns to go and talk to these people and sit with them and tell them what they were doing; and these old people said these visits were the best part of their day. At puberty, society makes an impact on the heart. Later there is more than that: When you become an adult, you feel no longer concerned with only one little part of society; you feel a responsible member of the world. Then you have the possibility of doing your part for the whole of humanity, not for one little part of it. So these are the phases, and how to keep the child's spirituality alive is by giving them the possibility to practice it.

Q. Is it possible to develop this latent spiritual behavior in every child? Some children never seem to learn; they go on scratching and biting, however much you try to teach them not to. They seem unable to have any feeling of kindness or any sense of obligation towards other children. Is goodness always there?

Mr. Montessori: There must be something wrong in the surroundings of the life of this child. After all, the behavior you describe is the general behavior of society nowadays, isn't it? The child lacks something which he should have and no amount of preaching will compensate for this lack. Preaching is like saying to a lamp which is out, "Hey, give out some light." You can try to persuade it, you can shout at it, but until you put on the current, it gives no light. It is not a question of appealing to consciousness in order to obtain something that is spiritual. The spiritual comes through continuous experience, and needs to be fed by the behavior of other people. I can assure you of this much: Here in London, there are a great many psychoanalysts that send children to the Montessori schools in order to have them cured; and they are cured because in this environment these things disappear in the only way they can disappear. Not by the magic of Montessori, but by providing normal surroundings and thus something that satisfies the spirit. That is all. It is not so much what is in the children, it is a problem of society. If society does not make it possible for them to develop it, then there is no possibility.

More and more people are trying to provide the right sort of surroundings, and this is a great consolation. In Bergamo, Italy, there is now a state institution to create trained assistants for baby care according to Dr. Montessori's methods. These are young ladies who study for about three years. They visit the mother before their child is born to give them the necessary instruction and also to prepare her spiritually for the birth of the child. They attend her at the time of the birth and help with the child during the first weeks, and are available for consultation for three years. So there are signs that the conscience of the adult begins to be touched.

Q. If the parent could decide there were places not only for things, but for feelings, it would help the child. Is it possible in our own life with our own children?

Mr. Montessori: In a lecture to a group of religious people and parents, Dr. Montessori said that from the very birth onward, religion should, in one way or another, enter the child's life. She herself, being a Catholic, always had a statue of the Virgin near the child, standing illuminated by a small light. This is something that is different from the child's ordinary surroundings, and when the mother passes there, she makes the sign of the cross or some kind of acknowledgement. The child absorbs the fact that this is very important and different from the rest; it should always have its place and always be respected. Dr. Montessori recommends it from birth; that is one of the ways to help children have this feeling.

Q. We as parents should provide an example for the child. There are things that I would not have in the house, even though they are found outside. In a Montessori school, are distinctions drawn between good and bad things? For example, I feel strongly about the futility of war and would not have things in the house which remind children of war.

Mr. Montessori: No, first of all, you will not find armaments and things of that kind in a Montessori school. If I found them, I would say the school was not worthy of the name Montessori. We bring into the life of the child those things which help him to develop normally, and certainly war is not a normal thing. The only trouble is that even if you don't give them toys, there are so many reminders of war all around that they absorb them just the same. But I would certainly try to inspire a horror of war rather than approval of it.

Q. Can the child recognize if the parent has a strong feeling even if nothing is said?

Mr. Montessori: Sometimes yes, sometimes no. But if there is something which is right, and which is expressed rightly, the child will take it, and it will be an example for him, and will help him.

Q. Is it desirable for the parent to isolate children from harmful influences by keeping them away from bad things, such as weapons, which they may grow to delight in, or should our influence be only by means of the inner attitude?

Mr. Montessori: There you can certainly have an influence if you start young enough. The child does not study your words, but if you have a deep persuasion, I am sure you can affect the child in the right way.

Q. I feel that the child is very much influenced by the love that is felt by the mother, even at the moment of conception. If that was lacking, is it possible for the proceedures of Dr. Montessori to repair the harm that has been done?

Mr. Montessori: I believe the experience of a normal life in a Montessori school will offset it. I do not know if the child will be as perfect as it would have been, but it will be greatly helped. We have had experiences of children who lacked love after birth as well as before, and even so attained equilibrium and were helped. Help can be given if the child comes to you at a young age; the older they are, the more difficult it is.

Q. Do you see anything in the Montessori method that can help adults? Through a change of environment is something still possible?

Mr. Montessori: You understand that the Montessori method basically is to influence the individual at the right moment of his life. If a child is nine years of age, he has certain tendencies. If he is five, he has certain other tendencies. If he is fifteen, certain other tendencies. The thing that you should know is what are the right tendencies of the children of that age. Through these, they can be helped.

Q.   Are these tendencies and psychic phases explained in the Montessori books on sale?

Mr. Montessori: Dr. Montessori's book, *The Secret of Childhood*, will give you a beginning, an indication. You have two children, two years old and five months. In this case, I can recommend two books: *The Absorbent Mind* for the five month old, and *The Secret of Childhood* for the older one.

Begin from Afar —
Gurdjieff's Approach to the Child

J.G. Bennett

Tonight I am going to speak to you about a specialized theme: that is, what I myself observed and heard and read about Gurdjieff's advice and practice in dealing with children. I say this is a restricted theme because Gurdjieff was concerned with the whole of man, and especially with the problem that we have to face in our adult life from the fact that our childhood did not proceed as it should have proceeded in accordance with the real needs of human nature. He almost invariably spoke of education, as we know it, as something almost entirely harmful to the essential nature of the child, and as resulting in an artificial being who has lost touch with his real self. Therefore the problem that we meet in our adult age is to rediscover the real self and repair the damage that has been done to us by a faulty education.

Now we come together tonight to speak about the other side of the picture, to see whether it is possible for us as parents and as teachers of children to prepare them for adult life in such a way that their true potentialities — which are limitless — should not be too much obstructed by our mishandling of them. I put it in this form because this is the emphasis that Gurdjieff placed upon our human situation: that we men are not in a natural situation. We do not start from the true starting-point for a man, but with a very severe handicap, a long way behind the starting point. This is not the result of a faulty education only, but also of the accumulated influences of wrong ways of living that mankind has followed for countless generations. One certainly cannot understand either Gurdjieff's teaching or his methods unless one sees that he looks at the human problem first as one of repair or restoration, and only afterwards as one of natural and full development. This applies to us in our adult age doubly, because on the one side we bear a hereditary burden and on the other, we carry with us the consequences of a faulty preparation for our mature life. Gurdjieff places special emphasis upon the inherited burden of man. This burden in its essence can be described by the one word "egoism." This egoism is associated with blindness, with illusion, so that man cannot liberate himself from his egoism — that is, his false attachment to an unreal part of himself — unless he can first liberate himself from the illusion that he is already a normal human being.

The illusion of normality results in our seeing — as Gurdjieff puts it — reality "upside down." Because of this, man in his life on earth tends to give importance to the things which are unimportant and to be unable to value the things that really do matter. This is not just a matter of knowledge — that a man should know the things that matter and even give an intellectual assent to the importance of higher, spiritual values — but rather that in spite of what he knows, he remains a prisoner of this state of illusion. One consequence of this is that he is unduly dependent upon the influences that surround him, particularly the influences of other people. We live in a ridiculous situation of minding all the time what other people may be thinking about us, what they may be saying about us, valuing ourselves not in terms of what we really are, but what we appear to be in the eyes of other people. We look for security and strength in that which is essentially perishable: that is, the material life of man — the life of his body, and the things that are associated with the bodily life — and fail to value the real part of ourselves, which Gurdjieff calls our real "I."

I would have liked to have read to you something from Gurdjieff's writings in order to express in his own words what he has to say about this, but those of you who have studied these writings at all will know that he expresses himself in a very special way, which cannot be approached just in one step. Wherever one picks up something to quote, one always finds that there are either very strange words which one has to study carefully in order to see what they mean, or else that he has strange ways of expressing things that at first even seem to convey quite a different meaning to the one that he intends. Therefore, I had to put aside this intention of quoting verbatim from any of his writings, as I suppose that there are comparatively few of you here who have studied them. There is one passage, at the end of the first part of *All and Everything: Beelzebub's Tales to His Grandson,* in which he speaks of man as being composed of three parts, each of which requires special and exactly appropriate education and preparation; and in addition to these, there is something else which he calls his real "I." Man who comes to adult life without his real "I" can be compared to a carriage with horse and driver but no master, and therefore no one to determine where the carriage should go or what it is to serve. Such a carriage can only become — as Gurdjieff puts it — a hackney carriage or a taxicab that can be hired by any chance passer-by. He therefore emphasizes that the real task of those who prepare children for adult life is to make it possible for them to acquire their own "I": that is, to be themselves in front of all their outer and inner life situations.

The parts of man that require to be educated and developed — and which Gurdjieff says are not normally developed at all under our present educational procedures — are not so easy to describe. I am not going to go into this part of Gurdjieff's teaching, his teaching about psychology, because that would not be possible in one evening's talk. I am going to speak now rather about his own procedures, dividing the needs of man into three parts: the bodily needs, the psychic needs, and the spiritual needs, as I did in the first lecture. The whole of Gurdjieff's procedure falls under these three headings, and in a certain sense, the three parts of man which have to develop do correspond to these three sides of man's nature.

Let us start with the bodily side. In Gurdjieff's own autobiographical writings, *Meetings with Remarkable Men*, he describes with approval the procedures of his own father, and also of his first tutor, as examples of how he thinks ideally a child should be brought up. He refers to two or three things about his father's procedure in relation to his body. For example, one should know one's own body, and should learn to be free from the kind of bodily fears that afterwards very much restrict one's ability to live life fully. He describes how his father used to make him get up early in the morning and go out and wash under the pump with cold water, even in the winter, when he was still a child. I have been in the Caucasus when it was forty degrees below freezing, and it is hard to believe that anyone would make a child do it. I doubt whether he expected as much as that of the child. Nor do I think Gurdjieff intends that we should gather from what he says that he recommends a very severe kind of bodily discipline for children, but rather that parents should not seek to shield their children from every kind of hardship. Another illustration that he gives is that his father used to take pains to make sure that he did not become squeamish about his body by putting things like frogs and mice into his bed, and that he should not be squeamish about the kind of food that he ate. Gurdjieff says that he ascribes a great deal of the strength that he had in later life to overcome great difficulties in his search for truth to these procedures of his father which, from his early years, helped him to be free from fear in relation to his body and to look upon his body as an instrument to be used and not as part of his own self.

Another point which Gurdjieff emphasizes is the need to instill in children the great importance of sexual purity. It should be impressed upon children that sexual impurity before adult life is reached can damage their higher possibilities of development. I have also heard Gurdjieff speak about this: that we should not, as parents and teachers, fail to make it clear to children that any kind of sexual impurity, particularly self-abuse or masturbation, is something that destroys possibilities and is very hard subsequently to repair. I know that there are people who have read Gurdjieff's books who have been really alarmed and depressed because they felt that their own childhood was not as it should have been and have wondered if they destroyed their own possibilities altogether. I have heard doctors argue this point with Gurdjieff because, as many of you know, the medical profession very often advises that masturbation is really not harmful to the body, and perhaps they say sometimes that it is even beneficial from a psychic point of view. I believe the doctors are wrong; but, no doubt, in speaking about this, Gurdjieff was referring not only to the bodily and psychic problems, but chiefly to the spiritual one. This is connected with the possibility for the child to acquire his own "I," to become himself. And he very often referred to the fact that boys and girls who have lost their sexual purity before the age of eighteen or twenty — or whatever it may be — find themselves later on in front of very great difficulties in their spiritual fulfillment. As he laid so much emphasis upon this —

and I frequently heard him speak about it — I certainly had to tell you about it as part of the account of his attitude towards the upbringing of children in respect to their bodily functions.

As regards the psychic needs of children, Gurdjieff put special emphasis upon the right feeding of the impulse present in all children to learn, to make, and to do things. He describes, for example, how from an early age he used to learn different skills, and how his father — as soon as he discovered that he had really acquired some skill — would deflect his attention from that and start him on something else. He might turn from learning about carpentry to learning about weaving, and so on. His aim was to make it clear that the ability to learn is something that can be acquired through training and that this is part of the psychic preparation. It is not the end point. It is not the specialized skill that is required, but the psychic flexibility, the psychic adaptability that comes from learning things that is important for the future life. This satisfies one of the essential psychic hungers of man and prevents this hunger from feeding itself on useless stimulations.

Another side of this feeding of the psychic needs of children is connected with the interest in what is strange and difficult to understand. I have seen him tell children things which were very surprising for children and have seen how this has left something behind which has been a preparation for an approach for the deeper and more spiritual problems of life. In that connection, I would like to refer to the title I chose for today's talk, "Begin from Afar." This was certainly one of the things Gurdjieff advised us very strongly: Never attempt to teach children directly about high and deep spiritual questions, including questions of religion. If we did so, they would only be taken as a psychic, mental, or emotional experience and would not really penetrate into the deeper understanding of the child. One should always, as he put it, begin from afar in such a way that their own search would be encouraged. What we do with children should be a response to their search rather than an attempt to instill or teach them anything. I refer of course to the deeper realities, not to the acquisition of practical earthly knowledge.

It seems as though Gurdjieff did attach considerable importance to interest in the wonderful, the marvelous: tales of travellers, tales of strange, unexplained events. My own experience and memories of my childhood certainly confirm that it is this kind of stimulus that served as a much more real and effectual preparation for my subsequent interest in deeper things than attempts to give me religious teaching in any formal way.

In short, the psychic hunger of children can be satisfied through the active development of their latent powers and through their own natural sensitivity to the wonders of creation. These are food for the psyche and they include all that is required for their preparation to live full and useful lives on the earth. All that is beyond this is unnecessary and only weakens the psyche and disturbs its normal equilibrium. I think that all that is connected with what Gurdjieff called "beginning from afar."

The third side — that is, the approach directly to the spiritual — can be understood only if you remember what I said at the beginning about Gurdjieff's conviction that our problem is not just that of a natural development, but of a putting right of something which is not right with man. For example, he spoke very often of what he called the 'illusion of will." The illusion of will is that man supposes that his desires and his impulses proceed from his own "I", from his own will; whereas in reality, they are only reactions to his environment. A man who has strong reactions is said to have a "strong" will, a man who has varying and vacillating reactions is said to be a man with a "weak" will. In either case their "wills" are no more than reactions and they do not — insofar as they are just reactions — come from their own "I." The question then is, how is the approach to be made so that this "I" that is latent in the child can come forward, enter into his consciousness, and occupy its right place as the ruler of his life? One side of this is connected with decision and responsibility.

This has a bearing upon our educational systems. Roughly speaking, I suppose we can say that there are nowadays two sorts of attitudes towards education. In the first, the teacher in effect accepts the responsibility, and results are obtained through the responses of the child to the responsibility that is taken by the teacher. What is expected of the child is conformity and obedience, preparedness to learn and if necessary to imitate. The other attitude emphasizes, on the contrary, the importance of developing the power of decision and freedom in the child, and leaves a great deal of freedom in the choice in the manner of working and, indeed, of whether to work or not. I think it is generally recognized that both these methods of education can give disastrous results, quite contrary to what is hoped for. This can be understood from something that I observed very particularly with Gurdjieff. Certainly he attached great importance to the child's power to decide for himself; but on the other hand, he confronted children with this very seldom, not at all as a regular procedure. He said that if a child were constantly expected to make decisions before it had reached the age of decisions — what he called "the responsible age" — this would only produce a state of nervousness, and even the failure to develop his own "I." Therefore, at comparatively rare intervals and in such a way that it would not be forgotten, he would put children in front of a decision and observe them. Afterwards he would show them the importance of having decided one way or the other. Having done so, he would leave this and not disturb the state of the child by constantly expecting him to decide matters which he was not yet ready to decide.

So it seems as if Gurdjieff's attitude towards these various educational procedures was that either extreme is bound to give the wrong result, and that it is on the whole better to follow the normal educational procedure — where the responsibility is taken mainly by parents and teachers — but not to forget that this will not by itself develop the real "I" of the child. This comes only through allowing the capacity for decision to develop spontaneously. He was particularly emphatic about not trying to reach this through any sort of sentimental or emotional approach.

I will tell you two little stories that illustrate this. I was present at Gurdjieff's last birthday party before he died in 1949. He was then in New York; his birthday was the thirteenth of January — or at least that was the day he said was his birthday — and there was a children's party held in the Wellington Hotel in New York, in a big suite with a particularly big room. The children of his pupils came from different parts of America. I suppose there were thirty or forty of them from three or four years old to fifteen or sixteen; I forget the ages. That morning he sent someone around to the bank to get a large number of silver dollars. He put a big tray on the floor and said to the children, "You can choose what you like, you can have either four silver dollars or one five dollar bill." And the children went and stood in front of it, and you could see that this was really a choice. The silver dollars were very beautiful, but the five dollar bill would buy a little more. Some chose one way, some chose another, some just could not choose at all. After this little demonstration of putting the children in front of a choice, a lady who was there spoke up. I should mention that he had the habit of calling his pupils that he knew best and was friendliest with by various queer nicknames. This lady was called "Crocodile." She had done a great deal of good work with the displaced children in Europe and brought many of them over and found them homes in America. She had just arrived that morning from Holland for Mr. Gurdjieff's birthday. So, as I said, she turned to him and said, "May I tell the children a story, Mr. Gurdjieff?" He grunted approval and she began telling them, in a very emotional voice, the story of two children that she had seen getting on the plane in Amsterdam the previous night, all alone, to come over to find a new home in America. And she kept on telling about these children travelling "all alone," and went on over and over again, and the children listened to it. When she had finished her story, Mr. Gurdjieff simply said, "In every language there is one phrase that all know: 'Crocodile tears.' " This illustrates what I mean by saying that there is one kind of wordless demonstration — by confronting a child with a situation — and there is the other way which attempts "to get something over" to the children. This he disapproved of altogether, because he said, "If you do this with children, if you try to 'get something over' to them, you are only increasing the great weakness of man: that is, his suggestibility and his dependence on others. You must simply put them in front of situations where they are able to learn."

Those of you who were here last week will remember how Mario Montessori spoke about the natural power which there is in children for work and effort and sustained attention, and how easily this is replaced by an automatism if we try to teach too much and do not allow their own powers to develop in front of a situation. On the other hand, he also emphasized the great need to create the situations for children in a right way, in accordance with their needs and with their own state of development. Everything that he said last week really so entirely agrees with what Gurdjieff taught that I would regard it as part of what I am saying. I would

like to add here in parenthesis that the Doctoressa
Maria Montessori had a high opinion of Gurdjieff, and she
invited me to go and speak about this particular question
at an education congress held in her honor in San Remo
in 1949.

I will tell you about another incident that illustrates
the capacity for a genuine effort that is in children.
Gurdjieff used to teach rhythmic movements and ritual
dances and so on, and in fact he was known to say of
himself that a "teacher of temple dancing" was his
chief claim to fame. It was an extraordinary procedure,
and those of you who have practiced these movements
know how very much is gained from them. When he had
classes for this work, he used to allow the children —
for example, those who were living at the Prieure in
Fountainbleau in the early 1920's — to come sometimes. They were usually the children of the people
who were practicing, and they were free, if they wished,
to imitate the movements from the side. After these
classes, Gurdjieff used very often to say to the people,
"Now you worked very well, you all come to dinner
with me tonight," and this invitation was of course a
great privilege for them. One evening the grandson of
one of his closest pupils and helpers and this boy's
mother were present in the class. When Gurdjieff invited
the people to dinner, the boy said, "Can I come?" Now
it happened that he had not done as he usually did:
that is, he did not stand and copy the older pupils in their
work. So Mr. Gurdjieff said to him, "No, you have not
worked like the others; if you want to come, you have
to earn it. Can you hold your arms out sideways? Like
this, for five minutes?" The boy said, "I don't know."
So Gurdjieff said, "If you can, you can come tonight."
And this boy — he was maybe eight or nine years old —
held his arms out. Now this is a very difficult thing for
anyone, particularly anyone unaccustomed, and especially so for children because the formation of the mus-

cles is not yet complete. The effort was certainly an-
tagonizing for the boy, and after three or four minutes
tears were running down his cheeks and he said, "Can I
put my arms down?" His mother and grandmother both
shouted, "Non!" He continued and saw his five minutes
out. It had a very powerful effect on everyone who saw
this. This was twelve or thirteen years ago and he is
now a young man with remarkable gifts and qualities.
I ascribe a good deal of what that boy has gained to
procedures of this kind. But you must understand that
they were used very seldom. I really must emphasize
this feature of Gurdjieff's handling of children: For
the most part, he would leave them alone, would almost
ignore them; but when he did intervene, it was always
something very definite that would not be forgotten.

Another side of this acquisition of one's own "I"
is not being closed to other people. You know, we find
it very difficult — even with our own children — to
be with them in such a way that they will remain open
to us and we remain open to them, and that there is a
real understanding between us. But it is not sufficient,
really, that children should know only their own family.
They need very much to know more than this because
there are different types of people, and they need to have
their natural understanding of types — which is inherent
in them — allowed to develop by contact with people.
I mentioned Gurdjieff's Institute in Fontainbleau, which
he started at the end of 1922 and which he kept going
for about seven years in different forms. I was there once
or twice for a relatively short period, and I saw the young
children there, some of whom I had met even earlier
in Istanbul. I met them again much later, when they had
grown up. Some I know still. What struck me particularly
about those children was that however diverse they
might be in what they were subsequently able to make
out of life, and in their own characters and qualities, they
had one quality unmistakably in common: a really

uncanny insight into people. Everyone of you who know any of these children who were brought up under those conditions will agree with me about this striking quality, and it is something that is really very much lacking in most people today. I do not believe that it is a rare thing that people should have the power of understanding what others are like, and how they are likely to behave. But it is very seldom given the chance to develop. These children who were present and saw the various kinds of procedures, very often appearing to be neglected, undoubtedly acquired this insight into people. As I said before, this is, in my opinion, connected with being ourselves. Partly, we know other people through knowing ourselves; but also, certainly, in part we know ourselves through the ability to recognize that people are different, and to realize that their behavior comes from something in them, and is not to be taken for granted.

I can not pretend to say that I can see how this was achieved — except by the fact, of course, that the children were living in a community and saw many different kinds of people, and also that they saw people working under conditions where it was clear that they were aiming at something that was beyond the ordinary values of everyday life. In those conditions more sides of people are exposed.

Maybe we could do a good deal more for our own children if we were prepared to expose ourselves more to them; this has been mentioned several times already in this series of lectures. For example, the importance of not pretending to children to be other than we are: that certainly Gurdjieff never did and never allowed people to do if he could help it. It is a great weakness that we should think it necessary to appear to be wonderful, or good, or clever, or something in front of our children. I think everyone who has seen the difference in relationship between parents and children knows how very much the confidence of children in their parents depends upon whether or not there has been any attempt to appear different from what one is.

Now I want to come on to the last part of this, and really the most difficult: and that is speaking about the theme of these lectures — the spiritual needs of children. I have mentioned Gurdjieff's *All and Everything or Beelzebub's Tales to His Grandson,* which is unfortunately so difficult that few people who have not been driven to it by a strong need have ever taken the trouble to study it. This book is really from end to end a treatise on education, because it describes the proceedure of the old devil, Beelzebub, towards his grandson, Hassein. The aim of this procedure becomes clear as the book nears the end, and that is to arouse in this boy, in this child — who corresponds to a human child of thirteen or fourteen years old — a sense of compassion towards mankind, and the desire to serve humanity. The final evidence that satisfied Beelzebub that his whole proceedure had produced the result that he wanted is when he sees his grandson weeping. When he asks him why, Hassein says, "It is because of the unfortunate situation of these beings that live on the earth and the difficulty that they have of escaping from the consequences of the past, and I made a vow with myself that I would devote my life to understanding this and to finding some way by which I could help them."

People who knew Gurdjieff only superficially from what has been said of him, or written by people who did not perhaps know him, fail to see that the strongest impulse in his nature was his sense of compassion for the situation of mankind and the urge that he had to do something — whatever might be in his power — to help people to become free from the illusion that holds us in that unfortunate situation of living our lives according to false values, or "seeing Reality upside down."

I think that, side by side with the things I have said earlier about the decision and sense of responsibility for oneself, the real self of man acquires its true quality through compassion. That is how I interpret both the way Gurdjieff lived his own life and what he taught in his books and in his procedures. It is, of course, necessary to make a distinction between compassion and sentiment. Sentiment — in the sense of sentimentality — is one of the ways in which illusion is fostered. People are prevented from seeing the truth about themselves or about the world in which they live by taking what they see in an emotional, superficial way. Therefore, just as Gurdjieff was so very insistent upon the importance of true compassion, he was equally insistent upon the disaster of any kind of sentiment or false feelings about man and his situation or about people. This second side of his behavior — of his procedures, rather — was very disconcerting for many people. In reality he was very much concerned to break down the veneer of sentiment, false good will, false hope, and false expectation that prevents man from coming in contact with what Gurdjieff called "conscience." This is the quality of the self, or "I" of man by which he is aware of spiritual realities. Conscience was for Gurdjieff the supreme glory of man, the Divine Spark, the "Representative of the Creator"; and its presence in a man entitles him to be called and to be the Son of God. And he was very sure that man must choose either to live by his conscience — or to live by the influences that act upon him from outside. Then he will be a slave of his own physical appetites, his psychic appetites, and so on. The only way in which man can become free is to find and to learn to live by his own conscience.

The question, of course, which we have to try to answer now is: Can we, as parents and teachers, do something about this situation? Here Gurdjieff turns the whole responsibility back to us. It is not what we can do to put things right for the children — their situation is very, very much better than our own because they have not got the double burden that we have to bear. What we can do, though, is to correct ourselves, and through correcting ourselves not only do our procedures towards our children change, but the consequences of our own nature will cease to be transmitted to them.

There is something strange about this, and I will try to explain it because I really believe this is true. I have real evidence of it, and if it is true, it is very, very important. I have no doubt at all that we all of us transmit to our children hereditary defects of character, or will, of the inner quality of the self — not only the defects that there may be in the body and the psyche. In a certain sense, all mankind is fallen into sin. I think there is no doubt that there is a real meaning in the doctrine of the Fall of Man; whether it is to be understood historically or not, the reality is there. This means, as I said at the beginning, that we are not at the right starting point. We carry with us an hereditary taint, an hereditary burden. This we transmit to our children because we accept to be as we are. We cease to transmit this if we cease to be as we are, and therefore, in changing ourselves, we also change our children. I have seen myself how a certain kind of defect of character, which can be traced back over two or three generations, has ceased to be transmitted at a certain point when one person in that chain of transmission has really liberated himself from that particular defect. And this is so striking that when you see that happen, you realize how much greater the responsibility to our children is in what we are rather than in what we do.

Our aim should be that the children of the future should carry less of a burden and that the world should be different from what it is now. I suppose that there is nothing more fundamental in Gurdjieff's teaching than this: that we can change the future of mankind if we will change ourselves. We cannot do very much — perhaps nothing at all — to change the present; very little indeed to change the immediate future. We can change what will come in future generations if we begin to liberate ourselves from these illusions, from these deep defects of egoism and false valuation which infect the whole of our human life. Therefore it comes to this: Whether we have to deal with children as parents or as teachers, our task begins with ourselves; and there is very much more benefit to be derived by children from what those in contact do to put their own house in order than what they attempt to do to put the child's house in order. As I have said, the child's house is still in a much better condition than our own.

Of course, that does not mean that there is no difference between one kind of procedure and another, and I have suggested in this rapid survey some of the ways I have seen Gurdjieff acting, about which I have also heard and read. In general, it consists in this: It is important that a child should know and respect his own body; it is important that he should value work for its own sake and that he should enjoy learning for the sake of learning, because this power will remain with him throughout his life if only he values it sufficiently; it is important that he should be ready when confronted with situations to take decisions for himself, but it remains our responsibility to protect him from undue exposure to the kind of strain which will only tend, if exaggerated, to produce psychotic conditions in the child. Therefore this kind of procedure whereby children are confronted with moments of decision should be followed very cautiously and sparingly. Further, we should not attempt to instill directly in children religious or spiritual truths, but rather should allow them to come towards them. We can do this by keeping alive in children the sense of wonder, and the realization of how much there is that cannot be known and cannot be understood far better than by trying to impress upon them the extent of our own knowledge, or of man's knowledge of the present time. We should make it clear to them that all that we know is very little compared with the great wonder of the world in which we live, and that the great part of it is not to be explained by our scientific procedures. As far as the truly spiritual nature of the child is concerned, the opportunity should be taken for helping them to develop the quality of true compassion; that is, a sense of the need of mankind and the desire to be able to do something for that need. Compassion should be fostered in such a way that it will at no time degenerate into sentimentality, and at no time will it overlook the fact that we, all of us, ourselves, are able to do very little.

Finally, the particular point of Gurdjiff's about breaking the line of transmission of hereditary traits, breaking the line of transmission of the burden of the past of mankind, is something very important. If this only could be understood, all of us as parents and teachers would feel our responsibility towards ourselves in a different way. In spite of our egoism, it is really easier for us to overcome, to be prepared to make sacrifices, if necessary, to liberate ourselves from our own defects for the sake of others rather than for our own sake. This is a very strange thing, but it is in my experience true – especially for the sake of our children; we may be too much caught in our habitual ways to be able to persist in perfecting ourselves for our own sake. There is undoubtedly in man – closely connected with conscience – a love of children which is almost universal. This can perhaps be the very greatest factor for changing man, if only we can understand how the love of children should be translated into a sense of responsibility for ourselves.

QUESTIONS

Q. I am in the position of observing the effects of
teaching on children, but I don't know what to look
for. Could you say something specific about that?

Mr. Bennett: You are in a position to observe the effect
of teaching upon children, but you don't know what
to look for to see if the procedure is in agreement
with what I have been saying. I would like to say something about the difference between the educational
procedure where the child is almost wholly passive
and the educational procedure where there is a genuine
response from the psyche of the child. This corresponds
to the first two parts of which Gurdjieff spoke: There
can be educational procedures which really do not touch
the inner nature of the child at all. He can, for example,
learn to read and write and to do arithmetic, go further
and pass exams and so on, almost exclusively by the
procedure of conditioning his reflexes. That means that
in reality this whole procedure is only working on the
physical organism and the nervous system, and the
psyche of the child is really left untouched. In effect,
he has not understood anything of what he has learnt
in that way, and all that remains after the educational
procedure is finished is simply techniques, and nothing
else. The techniques have really been acquired by the
conditioning of the nervous system. In order to have the
second kind of teaching, the kind of teaching where
there is an authentic response in the psyche, it is necessary that there should be an action from the child's
own psyche. In certain cases, this conditioning procedure
is much quicker than in other cases. Therefore it requires
a different arrangement of the educational practice in
order to make it work. This consists in providing some
psychological tests to ensure that the child has himself
recognized the difficulty he has to overcome. The child
must see when he does not understand and the teacher

must make the moment of "seeing" as the cue to his own response. Sometimes it is necessary to have a great deal of patience in order to wait so that a child will for one moment see what he has to understand — let us say the significance of a mathematical operation, or of the syntax of a foreign language. If that has not been understood, there will be no understanding of mathematics, nor any real possibility of entering into the spirit of the literature of that other nation that speaks the foreign language.

It can be said, roughly, that in every human being there is a capacity or power to react passively and mechanically which does not differ from the same power in animals. There is also a power to act positively, to stand up to the environment and so to "be oneself." It is this power that says, "I do not understand," or "I do understand"; and it is the development of this power that is essential in any true system of education.

We certainly can observe in educational procedures whether there has been an arousing of this second power, which Gurdjieff regards as the one that really matters for the development of the child. This power in the child can say "no" to what is offered to him, so that there is a clash of yes and no. If the child is actually able to say, "I do not understand," and if the teacher will listen and recognize that the child has said this — whether in words or simply by his actions — then that "I do not understand" is the awakening of the psyche of the child. From this, there will be able to be an action between the active and passive parts. From that action something will have been acquired which begins to be the child's own: understanding. I think it is possible to observe in educational procedures whether in fact that sort of contact is made, or whether it is not made.

As I say, from my own experience, this is not very easy in a fixed curriculum, because sometimes it takes time to reach this point of "no" which will afterwards lead to genuine understanding. And at other times, this "no" is extremely quick. The procedure can then be understood and the technique is then acquired so much more easily that a great deal of time is saved. Teaching in this way goes much more by jumps than the procedure which is simply one of conditioning, which is merely a matter of repetition in order to produce the same kind of action as Pavlov with his dogs. We must recognize that educational procedures are very often like Pavlov's conditioning of reflexes. Some which are considered to be effectual modern educational procedures are really based upon the conditioning process, merely simplifying it by making better use of our present knowledge of the human nervous system. But if we want to come to something different, there has to be what Gurdjieff called the "struggle of yes and no," without which there cannot be the birth of understanding.

We are concerned now with the deeper question of the spiritual need of the child. I think that Gurdjieff's point here is that first of all, this capacity for understanding has to be developed in the child during his early years, during what Gurdjieff called "the preparatory life." If this capacity is developed, then afterwards there will be something to respond to the deeper, spiritual realities. Therefore, we should not try to occupy ourselves with trying to do anything in that field, except perhaps in such a direction as I spoke about before, about compassion. I am trying to suggest that if you are simply observing educational procedures, you should look up this particular point, which you will find described in Gurdjieff's *All and Everything,* in the forty-sixth chapter, the one called "Form and Sequence."

Q. I am a teacher. Some of the things I heard tonight filled me with horror and cold fury. I am quite horrified to hear that Gurdjieff taught that masturbation is bad, when all the medical profession and the psychologists say that it is guilt over this sort of thing that causes complexes. And the boy who had to hold his arms out sideways for five minutes: Why not have compassion after three minutes when he begins to cry?

Mr. Bennett: I do not say that washing under the pump should be recommended as a practice, but there is something behind this which I do think should be observed; and that is the tendency to be afraid, not to know that our body has a far greater resilience and endurance than it will admit. In reality, the experience of people under extreme conditions, including children, shows that the human body has an enormous resilience and a power of endurance that must have some purpose in it. If we live only with a small part of this power, we shall not make full use of our lives. If children get into the habit of thinking that efforts are too much for them, or that it is dangerous if they do this or that, they are liable, all through their lives, to live only a half life. I think there is some truth in that.

Q. But why torture the child by making him hold his arms for five minutes?

Mr. Bennett: Think of the satisfaction of this boy when he had accomplished it. I saw it for myself, and it gave him a certain confidence that has remained. This is the way to a real self-confidence, because it is not mixed with a kind of egoism or pride. He knew that all the people around him could have done it.

The other thing that the lady objected to is Gurdjieff's speaking of the importance of sexual purity, and particularly the way in which he spoke of the dangers of masturbation. He said, and I said it myself in the lecture, that this is not at all the view of the medical profession or of psychologists, and that the current teaching on this theme is that if you frighten children about masturbation you will only give them complexes or fears, and that this will result in their situation being much worse.

I believe you are confusing the "guilt complex" — which is certainly to be avoided, Gurdjieff himself was very emphatic about this — and pointing out to the child that there is cause and effect. A child does not develop a guilt complex through learning that fire burns, nor need he do so by learning that masturbation weakens and may even cause grave danger to the power of understanding. If he cannot say "no" to the impulses of his own body, he will not be able to say, "No, I do not understand."

I cannot tell you how grateful I am to my own father that he contrived, at about the age of puberty, to convey to me that this was something unnecessary and would seriously damage my prospects for reaching a full kind of development. And I am quite certain that this did not produce any kind of complexes or anything of this sort in me; and I have always been thankful for it afterwards. Therefore I can speak for myself. I think that complexes and all the rest of it arise from the sort of thing that Mr. Williams was speaking about two weeks ago, when he was saying how we are afraid to talk to children about sexual questions. Clearly children should know all that needs to be known about sexual questions at a very early age, including the misuse of sexual powers. I see no reason to fear that trouble will arise from explaining to a boy or girl that masturbation is something that is harmful to the fulfillment of their possibilities. It is simply a matter of cause and effect. It does no harm, providing, as I say, it is not accompanied by any sense of mystery or shame about the sexual powers of man, or inability to talk freely with their parents or whoever they have to deal with about these things. That kind of secrecy or making a mystery of sex is clearly a most harmful thing, and I assure you that this was not one of Gurdjieff's failings.

I have myself often advised young men who have come to me for help with these questions. At times I have given them advice that was directly contrary to what doctors had told them. Years later they have come and said, "That was a wonderful thing for me, because I saw your advice was right and I followed it. It did not produce any of the reactions that I was told to fear." I personally believe that there is a great deal of blundering about this at the present time. I am glad you have said your part, because I would not like it to be thought that in reporting to you what Gurdjieff said and did on this subject, I am saying something that is generally accepted. But I would say, more is the pity.

Q. Gurdjieff emphasizes the importance of sexual purity up to the age of twenty. But these are some of the years when physically the sexual forces are the strongest of all, so the very strongest energies have no outlet.

Mr. Bennett: Gurdjieff did not say up to the age of twenty, he said up to "responsible age," which may be reached at eighteen.

Q. Even so, it is very hard.

Mr. Bennett: I am bound to say that, as far as Gurdjieff's procedures are concerned, it does seem to me that they hang together. For example, he told us that boys and girls, from childhood through puberty and onwards, should accustom their bodies to hard conditions. We have that in England, to a certain extent, in our sport, and that certainly has been a great help to many. I have been in countries where they had not got any organized sport, but there the children really work. For example, I was thinking of what I had seen in some countries of the Near East, where, I am quite satisfied, sexual impurity such as masturbation is not a trouble like it is in the Western countries. Maybe it is partly connected with our overfeeding, I don't know. Certainly in those countries the young people work very hard. From early childhood, they take part in the life of the family. Children are already looking after big animals, and their bodies are fully extended. By the time they reach puberty, they are doing hard physical work. I would like to mention here that, for example, sweating is connected with the whole of our physiological balance. Clearly man as an animal is intended to sweat, because he is provided with sweat glands, and if he does not, certain things fail to happen in his entire metabolism. When people live under the conditions I have been describing, their sweat glands are kept in a very healthy condition, the skin is kept in an active state. The result of that is that these things that you describe are not nearly so difficult to cope with.

You may retort, "Well, what are we to do about it? We live in a very artificial condition; very few people nowadays sweat at all, and if they do they do so only perhaps once a week, when they play games or something like that." But you must remember that man is a beautifully constructed physiological mechanism, and if we do not allow one part of this whole mechanism to work normally then the other parts will be affected by it. That is why I say that these procedures of Gurdjieff's which arouse such horror may also have some importance for the total physiological balance of the growing child, and especially through puberty. If we are not prepared to do anything to keep the full activity of the sweat glands, the skin, and so on through full exertion, then the problem is obviously aggravated.

Q. I have been a teacher for many years, and head-mistress for more years, and I left my job as head-mistress because I was not allowed to do what I thought was right for the children. I have now become a therapist, and I hope to put right what education has put wrong in children and adults. I do not think you have touched on the thing that can help tonight. The child is born with an innate power to do the right thing throughout his life if he is allowed to. Now from birth onwards, he is not allowed to do this. He is born in a hospital. He is not allowed to make his own rhythm. He is fed when the nurses think he should be fed, he is not allowed to be suckled by his mother, he is thwarted every moment of his life, until his death, almost. I did not see the child with my own eyes until ten years ago. I went through my college training, I saw children through the eyes of my teachers, my college lecturers, other adults. It was not until I went to a school for junior children that I suddenly saw a child and saw that we murder children through our educational systems. I have always wondered why the lovely spontaneity of a child was absolutely crushed and killed by the time he got to school, and then why it was crushed and crushed until his adolescence. He is a thing, just ready to sit in front of the television and view what other people tell him. And when I really saw the child for the first time, I knew that here, in the child, is all the direction that the child needs from birth if we allow him to be himself. That is, give him protection for the first years, the mother and the father both to minister to the child, to give him security, never to be left to cry. The heart-broken cry of a child will be the heart-broken cry of the adult who does not know what to do. He needs protection, and needs to be creative in his own way; he needs to crawl, to explore, to play with dirt, to do all sorts of things until he is ready, at about age seven — the first octave — to receive lots of help from other people. From seven to fourteen he should learn through his play. In the first few years, he can solve every emotional problem for himself, without help from anybody, through his play.

I would like to give you just one illustration: A child did nothing but tear up things for two years. He just tore up everything that was given to him and he was allowed to. At the end of that time, he wanted to do some drawing; he did some drawings of bombs. At the end of that time, he wanted to do clay, and he wanted to squeeze, and I said, "What are you squeezing?" He said, "My father, because he will not let me make a mess." He always wanted to make a mess. Well, when he had been allowed to make a mess for two years, he wanted to begin to learn. Now I asked the mother, "Was this child in the bombing?" "Oh, yes." she said, "We had a direct hit, and what a mess." The child knew his own way out. With education, he would have just become an imbecile. I could give you instance after instance. The child can solve his own problems if only the adults will observe him and keep away from him.

I agree with Gurdjieff that education takes a man away from his real self, and I, an educator of many years experience, would like to see it wiped away, quite clean away, and let people become real. But I think you should know about this power in the child, and you have not mentioned it. I wonder why?

Mr. Bennett: I am sorry; when I used the word "conscience," I was referring to this power. I think that when Gurdjieff spoke about "beginning from afar," he meant you must not interfere. You must have much more respect for the child than to try to pump things into it. I thank you very much, because what you said sounds much better than what I said.

Lecture 5

The Taste of Reality —
Dr. Rudolf Steiner and the Child

Rev. Adam Bittleston

Children notice each other to varying degrees. Some children far more than others are aware of what the children in their environment are going through, and are prepared to do something about it. Others have their attention concentrated far more on the adult world and their own occupations, to some extent to the exclusion of other children and young people around them. Rudolf Steiner seems to have been a child who was very much involved in the needs of other children. He was a member of a very poor household, with acute needs, and in his school life he constantly had the task of trying to help the mentally retarded children in the same age group as himself. In his student days, he had the difficult task of teaching in a family where a boy was so retarded that it seemed ordinary education was impossible for him, and the young Rudolf Steiner was able to bring him — through great care and patience and love — to the point that this boy could go through the whole training for medicine and become a doctor. And then it seems as if for quite a long period of his life he had outwardly not much to do with children. He was engaged in building the work of the Anthroposophical Movement in other fields.

It was not until 1919, when he was fifty-eight, that Dr. Steiner had another opportunity to be active in education, and he seized this with enthusiasm. He became the advisor in the Waldorf School in Stuttgart, which very soon established an outstanding reputation in German education. In this school he would not only spend many long evenings and nights in discussion with the teachers, but he knew the children personally and was constantly occupied with their problems and their progress. At the end of his work, there came the opportunity to develop the field that had concerned him so much in his early life — work for severely handicapped children. In 1924, less than a year before his death, he gave a fundamental course of lectures on work for handicapped children — children, in his own words, "in need of special care." In England, this has become one of the best known fields for the application of his ideas.

All through his life, Dr. Steiner did something which I think is of importance to every one of us: He actively remembered his childhood. When I say remembered, I mean more than just looking back and recalling that this or the other thing happened. For him, remembering was a far more intensive activity. He suggested that we not only think what happened, but really feel ourselves again in the situation of early childhood, boyhood, and so on; to feel the colors and smells, the mood of the environment, to be transported back again into the situation. And he must have done this throughout his life. In his own autobiography, *Mein Lebensgang*, we find a tremendously vivid picture of his childhood in the country in Austria, and when he guided teachers it was often with these memories close at hand.

Dr. Steiner could also do something very rare: He was able to look at children and observe the transformation that goes on as they grow up in the part of themselves which is not visible to our physical senses. He gave, as the foundation for his educational work, a description of these fundamental changes as his supersensible cognition revealed them. When we are confronted with these descriptions, we may remember intensively, and give flesh and blood to these descriptions by recalling what life was like when one had to look up to everybody, instead of meeting them on a level, and when we had a condition of consciousness really very different from the one we have now.

I would like to describe to you a few aspects of these basic periods as he saw them; not trying to define the changes at the crucial turning points, but rather bringing a few examples of how we can approach the child between birth and seven years old, between seven and fourteen, and also, very briefly, from fourteen onwards. Do not imagine that I am describing an abrupt and complete change at a particular birthday. It is a gradual transformation, which is like a birth in the invisible part of man. Parts of each change may well come earlier, and others later, than the age which serves as a standard.

Let us look back on this very first period of childhood. Can we speak of there being a spiritual hunger in the child between birth and the age of seven? I believe that in this period, physical hunger is a spiritual hunger. The human being is so deeply devoted to the physical world in which he is trying to achieve a standing that everything physical is still felt as having its source in God. When a child is eating, this eating is a far more serious matter than eating is for the grown human being. For the child, taste is not only something in his mouth, but it goes down to his fingertips and to his toes. It is a profound and earnest experience, and so it is with all the other physical concerns of the baby or the young child. The grown-up constantly fails the child if he does not feel the importance of everything physical in this age. A fundamental duty in the treatment of young children, and in the treatment of the handicapped child, is reverence for small things.

Take the example of toys. I have looked through a great toy shop, from ground floor right to the top and down again, and I was only able to find one toy that seemed to me right for a child. A toy should be something in which a child experiences the materials of the world in their real qualities; experiences wood, for example, or some other true stuff. If a child has to do with a toy made of a superficial, unreal material — perhaps some plastic material — he is confronted with something which already deprives him of the taste of reality. A child should have as toys things that are in some way archetypal, are of the everlasting things. In a toy shop, I asked, "Do you ever have Noah's Arks nowadays?" They said, "Sorry, there is no demand for them." The child's hunger is to experience in the physical world the abiding realities. What sand is, what mud is — such things are much more important for the child than a plastic atom-rocket.

There are many other ways in which the child at this time can realize that the grown-up person appreciates the wonder of the physical world, the world about which the child is trying to learn. We can think of grace at meals, for instance. This is something so natural and right for the child. Have you ever seen in the child who is used to grace at meals the shock and the feeling of deprivation when it does not happen? The grace must of course be sincerely meant; then it is of great value, particularly in this first age when comparatively little should be brought as direct *teaching* to the child. The child learns at this time from the adult himself: what the adult is, how he speaks, how he moves. The child needs to feel, "I am secure in the genuineness and the goodness of what is around me."

I was haunted at one moment in my childhood, when I was about six years old, by the feeling of the different qualities of light; the difference between artificial light and sunlight. I felt, "Perhaps one night the gaslight will go on and no sunlight will come, no real daylight will come." A child needs to feel that what surrounds him, in the qualities of the grown-ups, is like daylight. In this security he can develop his own essentials. This security is fundamentally composed of two parts. On the one hand is the certainty that life around him has a form on which he can rely: meals are at a definite time, some things are permitted and some things are not permitted, and so on. On the other hand is the feeling that his individuality, his own self, is respected. Even the smallest children have a strong sense of dignity, and I think we should never humiliate the sense of dignity of the small child. Behind the small child is already the mature individuality. Sometimes, from the child's eyes, this already looks out at us, and always we should respect it: It may be an individuality much wiser and greater than we are ourselves. In this security of being held in a framework that can be relied upon, but being at the same time respected, the child can develop the great powers which have to be developed in this period − walking, speaking, and thinking. Dr. Steiner described again and again the significance of these acts in their greatness and their holiness. Never should the adult feel impatient about these developments, hurrying them on. They must come in the child's own good time. We should not have forgotten what it feels like to jump, for instance − the glorious sense of freedom when the child, who a short time ago could only crawl, can throw himself through the air.

At six or seven comes the time when something has become free in us that enables us to learn. Our thinking has reached the point at which our immediate environment does not satisfy us. We want to know more, to reach out beyond this immediate environment which at first presented us with such tremendous problems. Now we have the wonderful time of education as it should be − between approximately seven and fourteen − when thinking has not yet died. Dr. Steiner spoke about this again and again: We must realize — not in a sentimental way, but simply as a fact — that our thinking, the thinking that is dominant in the world today, is dead, as dead as a skeleton. When we teach a child before the years of adolescence, it is our responsibility to see that thinking has not yet died, and we must not burden the child with the results of dead thinking, the accumulation of inert information. What should be brought to the child between seven and fourteen are seeds that will grow through life, thoughts that have not come to an end but which will develop in later periods of life far beyond what can be consciously taken hold of by the child when he receives them.

I would like to give the example of religious education during this period because I think it is more relevant to your course here, and I cannot possibly give an adequate description of the whole curriculum advised by Dr. Steiner. Religious education begins in a way that is still linked with the first experiences of childhood: experiences of God in the physical world, in substance, in wind and light, in the flowers and animals. There is a passage which is quoted in Charles Davy's book, *Towards a Third Culture* (a book which touches fundamental problems of education today); it is taken from the late Dr. Sherwood Taylor: "On a clear, sunny autumn morning, I had walked into the gardens of St. John's College, Oxford. The dahlias were still in bloom and the Michaelmas daisies were covered with great butterflies—tortoiseshells, fritillaries, and red admirals. Suddenly, I saw the whole scene take on a new figure; every plant assumed a different and *intelligible* pattern, an individuality with a meaning that was the plant itself, which, by existing in that pattern was turned towards God and praising Him. So with the butterflies; they were not merely lowly organisms but intensely alive, clad in the livery of God, and in a fashion more personal than the plants were praising Him too. The world was a prayer, and I, fallen man, was the only being whose prayer was weak and broken. For there was nothing in my heart but love and tears and the avowal: 'Lord, I am not worthy.' Then I knew what was meant by 'Oh ye works of the Lord, bless ye the Lord, praise Him and magnify Him forever,' for I saw that praise."

The teacher needs to have this sense of reality, the sense that nature is always praising God, when he speaks about nature with the child. It is really a superstition of our time that only organisms with a nervous system can be conscious. We communicate best with organisms that have a nervous system – not always very well, but to some extent. We fail to reach the consciousness of other elements in our universe so well, but it is there. The element of joy and sorrow is really everywhere. As described in the passage above, it is **through** this consciousness that the meaning of all beings in their relationship to the Ground of existence is to be appreciated. The teacher needs to be able to describe the world of nature with this as his constant background; not as a theory, but in the mood with which he describes plants and animals, the earth, and the world of the stars. For the period between seven and about nine or ten, this can be the main theme in religious education. Perhaps teachers from many different points of view are feeling their way towards this task, which is very difficult to fulfill. We ourselves are much too blind to see the things of nature continually with this freshness, but we can learn from Dr. Steiner to understand better and better that it is the truth.

At first, the child hungers and thirsts for the divine in the world of nature. Gradually – as the child learns his own loneliness, his own solitariness in life – he needs to feel destiny, too, as a field where the divine works. This is the next task for the teacher: to bring the child as he approaches adolescence the sense that, "in the events of life I can see wisdom at work, a wisdom that comes with a friendly gesture towards me." There is so much in the world today that does not come with a friendly gesture, but with a profound threat to all human existence, and the child needs to be deeply reassured by the description of human lives in which the sense of leadership, of destiny, is apparent. Gradually there can come to the child a strong sense of having already an experience of the earth behind him. Today there is a danger that the idea of reincarnation comes — in wider and wider circles — in a very crude and external form. It can come in a form that simply puts before people's minds a string of human experiences from birth to death, following one upon another without any real direction or meaning. If this idea were to become general, the human situation would not be better than when the single life is the limit of consciousness. It would be worse. Only if the conception of reincarnation is gradually assimilated into our culture as a conception in which we can see the creative justice of God at work can it be a healing element.

And so, in the leadership of the child, reincarnation and destiny can become real experiences, real certainties, backing up a confident and courageous approach to life. Side by side with the gradual understanding of destiny, the child is led to the figure of Christ: Christ as the Being who brings the joys, and the Comforter in the sorrows of existence. It should not be too soon, but from about the age of nine the conception of God in all things should lead to a growing understanding for the figure of Christ Jesus himself, as a Being whom we grow to understand inasmuch as we individually are taking up responsibility for our lives. At the time of adolescence, the taste of reality can come to the child if we succeed in bringing the central mysteries of Christ's Being, and of the Eucharist, to him in freedom: not as a traditional dogma, but as something into which he can grow as an experience. Through this it may be possible for him to see, at times, the abiding light behind the visible light.

From adolescence onwards, we must leave a very great freedom to the child. All sorts of intellectual and moral somersaults will be taken in the next years, and we should not be too agitated about them. We should be confident about the young boy or girl, man or woman, and believe that the immortal being, of which we perhaps caught certain glimpses in early childhood, is still in charge and will guard against evil. As part of the human environment, our task is to go on believing, go on being concerned, go on forming a reasonable and steady background which can be called upon in times of need. In this period of life, something that belongs to the eternal spirit is coming into violent contact with the materialistic world — civilization as a whole. On the one hand, the young human being wants to share in everything that is going on in the world, and can share in it more and more. And yet he or she is not really just a creature of this time, but shows the effects of that period of existence in which we are in the spiritual world. The innermost soul is waking up, is struggling into expression more and more strongly, and is in the greatest tension and polarity in its relation with the externalities of present-day life. Here there must be thunderstorms. We should not feel that these thunderstorms are only destructive, though at this time wounds will be given and probably received in contact with the adult. Something is approaching which is of immense significance. The master of the ship is taking the helm into his own hands.

Now it is necessary for us to meet the young human being as we are, in all our limitations, without any pretensions, without any claims as far as authority and leadership are concerned. It would burden the child too much if we were to appear like this earlier: For the young child, we have to be leaders and guides and teachers. Now we must be willing to abdicate very thoroughly and only have whatever honor or leadership is given us. For what grows up now into maturity, what takes control, needs to meet us on a completely equal level. If we have done, in the first stages, what we sought to do, then we can be really confident, really happy about what is going to happen later. We can begin really to receive as well as to give, in practical cooperation.

What is it that we have tried to help the child to meet? What do I mean by the "taste of reality?" I mean something that is very familiar as a Christian doctrine, but which, in recent centuries, has become far too much simply a doctrine and not an experience. When we are aware of the holiness of the substances of earth and of the body of man, what is it that we are beginning to feel? It is what both exoteric and esoteric Christianity in their different ways have known as the Father, Ground of the World. When, through the experiences of destiny, the child comes to feel the Christ as Lord of destiny, as the giver of the joys of existence, as the comforter in the sorrows of existence, then the human being experiences God the Son. From adolescence onwards, through the storms, through this period in which continual reversal, tremendous antagonisms and releases from antagonisms are bound to occur, there approaches the experience of the Healing Spirit.

It is for union with the divine that the human being hungers and thirsts. The work of God is revealed in what the New Testament calls, in the Greek, "diakaiosyne." "Righteousness" is an inadequate translation. I have ventured to use the phrase "creative justice." If we use this phrase, which is nearer to the original meaning, we can apply to the children of the present day the words of Christ Jesus in the Sermon on the Mount: "Blessed are they who hunger and thirst for the creative justice of God." It is the lasting responsibility of the adult world to foster the fulfillment of Christ's promise which follows, and to avoid, in every way possible, hindering its fulfillment: " For they shall be satisfied."

QUESTIONS

Q. You mentioned reincarnation and you mentioned the Christian idea. How do you reconcile those two?
Rev. Bittleston: Many years ago, I knew a young man who was training for the Christian priesthood. At about the age of twenty-two, he came very clearly, simply from his theological studies, to the conviction that it is simply not possible for mankind to absorb what it needs to absorb about the Christ unless we have more than one opportunity to do so. Christianity is a much bigger thing than any existing or traditional church. It is something which we shall go on learning, and where we shall be joined in our attempt to learn by members of other religions, too; that is already beginning to happen. We shall then see that the Eastern teaching about reincarnation needs to be amplified by a Christian element. Sri Aurobindo, who died a few years ago in India, was already doing this to a very great extent. He spoke of reincarnation not in the sense of something simply laid on man as a burden because of his past wrongdoings, but rather as an opportunity for development towards the spiritual reality which comes to meet him. It does not seem to me that there is any conflict in the Gospels themselves or in the fundamentals of Christianity with the idea of reincarnation as an opportunity for the soul's growth. None of us complete our growing within a single life; the earth is given to us as the great opportunity for acting in freedom, where the immediate vision of the divine is cut off from us. Here on earth we can go on growing if it is the Will of Heaven to give us renewed opportunities to meet the problems in which we have once failed, and master them. It is quite extraordinary how among children today this becomes so natural; for even with quite small children you find it almost as their common sense. It needs interpreting and supporting. If I may give an example: A friend of mine had a son who

sent this message to his new-born cousin: "I hope she has gotten over being born all right." My friend and I said to each other, "Well, a lot of people have never got over being born!" The natural feeling of the child is, "I have come from somewhere already." Christ spoke of reincarnation not as something easy, but as something that had to be won. The recognition, for example, that in St. John the Baptist the soul of Elijah had come again to earth: something that could be earned by human spiritual endeavor.

Q.   May I suggest Leslie Dixon Weatherhead's books about reincarnation would help here — *Life Begins at Death,* for example.

Q.   How would you introduce the idea of reincarnation to children?

Rev. Bittleston: I believe that we can approach it through the problem of the apparent unfairness of fate; the extraordinary differences in human situations. There are people who at birth suffer such severe handicaps that their life is burdened from the very start. We should not attempt to explain this as a kind of punishment for past acts, but as tasks that have been undertaken by the soul, which will bear fruit in the future. When Christ Jesus was asked about the man born blind, he said that his blindness was not the consequences of his parents' sin or his own, but was for the manifesting of the glory of God. In the Gospel story, we see this manifestation in all the man did — not only in the endurance of his infirmity, but in the healing of it and in the witness that he afterwards bore. Now, for many handicaps no full blossoming may be possible within this life. For instance, we have schools for handicapped children, children whose lives cannot be very long and are bound to be very limited. But we can understand a great deal about them if we realize that this is a preparation for something great and significant. Children in general have a very strong feeling for this sort of fairness; it is not fair that somebody has to have all the misfortunes and somebody else all the good fortune. There must be an effective fairness, a productive fairness working in life. This is something very natural for children to feel. I do not think we should ever say, "This is our teaching and you should accept this," but rather try to see how the natural learning of the child leads to this. When they know that some people on earth think like this, then they are very open to hear more and to weigh it themselves in their feelings and their observation.

Q. Children in non-Christian countries have just as much spiritual hunger. Can Steiner's method help if there is not a Christian background?

Rev. Bittleston: Yes, one example has already arisen. It is perhaps most practical if I give an actual example. A few years ago, an important Jewish body approached an old friend of mine about the care of orthodox Jewish handicapped children, and said to him, "We have heard what Rudolf Steiner has done for handicapped children. We want our children brought up as orthodox Jewish children should be, but we want your help in dealing with their handicaps." I have visited this home where the children are receiving the help which can be given in this way without infringing upon the faith which their parents ask of them. Indeed, in the Rudolf Steiner schools for normal children, it is absolutely clear that religious instruction can be given in the school by the clergy of any denomination. If we have the opportunity one day to start a school in Cairo, for instance, we hope the appropriate religious teacher would come and help with the religious instruction. I believe that fundamentally it will be found possible to adapt the sequence that I tried to describe to the Moslem environment. Fundamentally, Christianity is not just a matter of Christian denominations; you will find that every religious movement in the world today is concerned with the being of Christ. The being of Christ can be found, as I once experi-

enced, in a purely Jewish environment, or in any genu-
inely religious environment. He can be found, whatever
name people give Him, even if they do not name Him at
all. The being of whom I am trying to speak is not limited
to any particular faith; indeed, the faith that names Him
may sometimes be His greatest obstacle, because of the
hardening that takes place in every religious body.

Q. Is it humiliating to the child to smack him?

Rev. Bittleston: That is a very good question. It can
be very humiliating. The child may well feel ashamed of
the grown-up, and probably the grown-up can feel
ashamed of himself because, generally speaking, if it has
got to the point of smacking, then something has gone
wrong. The child may, on the other hand, sometimes
feel his own need for a smack, and then he goes out of
his way to make the grown-up smack him. It is not then
humiliating, because the child and the grown-up agree
that the situation could only be solved in that way.
Always, when we smack a child, we should look back
over the course of events and ask: "Need we have got to
that point? Have we not really made a blunder, perhaps
quite a long way back? Can we put that blunder right?"

Q. One has to work it out in each case. Do you agree?

Rev. Bittleston: Yes, it can be very humiliating and
really an offense against the individuality of the child.
It is very important, if it does come to that point, that
we try and make it good by bearing in mind particularly
strongly that we are faced with a spiritual being who may
well be greater than ourselves, and in any case is something we must honor and revere. In this way, we can
make good to the child this momentary lapse on both our
parts. These things are of course not as simple as they
sound. I come from a country which uses far too much
corporal punishment — Scotland. It is a great defect in
Scottish education at the present time that there is too
much intimidation of the children. Corporal punishment
is given for faults in learning, which should never happen.

If there has to be corporal punishment, it should be for faults in discipline, but not for faults in learning. If I may add this: Altogether we have gone wrong when we put negatives before a child. We have to go back a bit and see why we had to say, "Don't." If we had to say "don't," the fault must be a bit in us, and not only in the child. If we had the right strategy, it would not have been necessary.

Q. I would like to come back to what you said about toys. Don't you think children often enjoy something made especially for them, even if it is not finished? If they have seen it made, and know it is made for them, they like it better.

Rev. Bittleston: I agree. Altogether toys should not look too finished, and the child should be able, as it were, to develop the toy in his own imagination. For instance, dolls: A doll you have made out of wood or out of stuff is far more valuable for the child than a beautiful one that squeaks "Mama" and so on. The child wants to use his capacity to make something great out of a rough-hewn thing, a thing that leaves opportunities open for imagination. A toy should not be a closed, finished thing. Big toys are also very good for small children — to have something really massive with which to deal.

Q. Certain types of stories help children in this respect. Children are aware that they have already come from somewhere. Fairy stories about search seem to hold them in an entirely different way. I mean stories that have a real meaning, not random stories.

Rev. Bittleston: I think you have touched on something very important indeed. In the period of religious education which I tried to describe to you, particularly the period between seven and ten, the stories which are true myths, true symbolic expressions of the soul, are immensely important. Children have a good feeling for the difference between a real fairy story and what you call — I think it is a very good expression — a random story.

They have the feeling, "This has the taste of reality."
Grimm's stories, for example: Grimm really had a right
instinct for the old true stories. These fairy stories came
from centers of deep wisdom where esoteric Christianity
was cultivated in the Middle Ages. A friend of mine,
Rudolf Meyer, has written wonderfully about the wisdom of these Grimm stories, how exact their pictures
are. And I believe that mothers will come to learn more
and more the great difference between genuine fairy
stories and stories produced (I think I had better not
name names) by some best-selling ladies. This is a difference between something that nourishes us for our
whole life and a synthetic creamy drink which only
leaves us with bubbles inside. But we need to believe
the truth of a fairy story in telling it. Most of us have
a great deal to learn about the things that can be brought
to children. They have so eager a mind to hear what we
say when we tell them stories of any kind. We are responsible, just as much as the mother is responsible for the
goodness of the food given to the child.

Q. As time goes on, children often lose what they have.
Do you think that this type of story, if it is fed to them
until they are twelve or older, will help them to hold
onto this until they can try to do something about it for
themselves?

Rev. Bittleston: Yes, of course. The Gospels also give
this taste of reality, and I think it is important for children in the later period to come to feel that what is contained in the Gospels is different from any kind of
thought-out legend or modern story simply told as a
story — to feel that here we have an approach to the
deepest realities of life, upon which we can rely.

Q.   As a small child, I can remember my admiration
for these tales: Cinderella, the Sleeping Beauty, Jack
and the Bean Stalk, the stories of Grimm, and the mira-
culous life of Christ. Other stories never seemed to stay
with me. The faces of the children I teach now are spell-

bound when they are listening to Cinderella or the Sleeping Beauty. Children can distinguish for themselves between stories that have value and stories that haven't. Rev. Bittleston: When we speak with children, we should realize that they receive with our words much more than simply the meaning of what we say. They receive with our words the whole background of our being; they take in what is really living in us. Dr. Steiner said that illnesses can appear in later life which are the result of a teacher's one-sidedness thirty or forty years ago. If a teacher has been, for instance, bad-tempered, violent, then this violence goes right into the body of the child. If a teacher has been phlegmatic and inert, this goes again into the being of the child and comes out in later life. When one faces this, it is almost overwhelming, we feel we cannot help giving some things that are inadequate for children, and that is true. We can believe that the children will make the best of what we give them if we go on trying to work on ourselves. That is really the fundamental thing to satisfy the spiritual hunger of the child — that the grown-up does not stop working upon himself, that no day does he stop working on himself. We can learn until the hour of our death; that is something that people today do not recognize enough. Right to the hour of death we can go on learning, every one of us. It is so immensely important for children to feel that the grown-up is not static, is not fixed and finished, but that something is happening in him, too.

Q. In tending to these deep needs which arise at various ages and stages, does it matter whether the influence comes from the father or the mother?

Rev. Bittleston: That is a very big and wonderful question. Goethe said, "I have from my father my stature and life's earnest guidance; from my mother my joyous nature, and the delight in telling stories." The mother has an immense sheltering task in the first seven years, and what I said about the material as something divine applies very particularly to the mother. The mother should not be disgusted by anything about the child, but should really give the child this sheltering wonder and delight. Generally speaking, the father's responsibility in the first seven years is a little more remote, to act as a kind of outer shelter. But he should welcome and lead on initiative in the child, freedom and initiative. And certainly his activities can be particularly important in the period between seven and fourteen, when the approach to destiny becomes acute. The father who could help his children to understand destiny would be a very good father. Someone who could help the children to feel, "You have each your own task, and I welcome that task." As Goethe says, *"Des Lebens Ernste Fuhrung"* — the deep line of a life, the intention of a life. Children should see in the father, particularly, a clear intention and a purpose, and in the mother a sheltering love. But now, in our complicated modern existence, it often falls to the mother to play a fatherly part, and to the father to play a motherly part. This can be very good indeed if both can manage it. We need to grow into all-round human beings, and to be people who can fulfill unexpected tasks.

Lecture 6

Children Taught of the Lord

A.I. Polack, M.A.

There is a famous rabbinical emendation of a phrase in
the fifty-fourth chapter of Isaiah which gives a glowing
account of the New Jerusalem, the ideal holy city of the
future. The original text ran as follows: "And all thy children shall be taught of the Lord and great shall be the
peace of thy children." The Hebrew word for "thy children" is *banayieh*, but with typical ingenuity an early
commentator noticed that by the alteration of a single
vowel — and we must remember that the parchment texts
were entirely consonantal — you get *bonayieh*: "thy
builders." Therefore, it might read, "All thy builders
shall be taught of the Lord and great shall be the peace
of thy children." In other words, according to this
rabbi what Isaiah really said was that if you are to produce the ideal society of the future, the society in which
children can thrive and express their personality in the
atmosphere of *shalom* — which means not only peace but
human welfare — those who are its architects and creators
must be "taught of the Lord": that is, spiritually minded
people. So that what we are really considering, as has
been shown in previous lectures, is how the spiritual
hunger of the modern child can be satisfied through the
influences which are brought to bear on him by those

who control his environment: by parents in the first instance, then school teachers, and finally through all the agencies that are operating so powerfully in the modern world on the young child and his development. Are these influences doing the job or doing it at all adequately? If not, and I quote from a previous lecture, "It comes to this: Whether we have to deal with children as parents or as teachers, our task begins with ourselves; and there is very much more benefit to be derived by children from what those in contact do to put their own house in order than what they attempt to do to put the child's house in order." I would profoundly agree with this judgment.

That the child has a spiritual hunger is implicit in the title of this series of lectures and cannot be questioned by anyone who has had anything to do with children. Whether or not it is true to say that "heaven lies about us in our infancy" — and my own view is that here there is some confusion in Wordsworth's poem between innocence, which is amoral, and spirituality — as the child's awareness and potentiality increase, there is at the same time a growth of the spiritual appetite. A sense of right and wrong develops very early and often quite independently of the norms of human conduct by which he is surrounded. It is a curious thing that all the time I was a schoolmaster I never once punished a boy who complained that he had not deserved the punishment. I would hazard a guess that a great deal of modern delinquency is basically due to a spiritual urge which finds no satisfactory outlet in conforming to established ways and conventions, and finds fulfillment in opposing them. The old principle *corruptio optimi pessimi*, the corruption of the best is the worst, holds as good today as it ever did, and how much of the "corruption" is due to the effect of adult influences on the child during his most receptive years!

If, then, it is *our* generation that needs to put its

house in order, its builders, according to Isaiah's view, must be "taught of the Lord." Only then can the welfare of children be secured. From the prophets onwards, Judaism has had some specific and significant things to say with regard to the best techniques which can be employed in the training of young people and the creation of a better world society. It has been saying them for close on three thousand years — we were reminded of this in the talk "The Lord's Song in a Strange Land" — and the sad thing is that they have rarely been heeded. But Judaism remains an angry young religion, and it will continue to say them until the Messianic time when "the earth is full of the knowledge of the Lord as the waters cover the sea." Some of the aspects of Hebraic teaching or Hebrew genius relate specifically to our subject of how we are to meet the challenge of youth and its spiritual hunger, and offer certain specific remedies for the besetting maladies of our time.

First I would put the Jewish emphasis on the practical — you might even say the pragmatic — as opposed to the theoretical. Judaism, like Confucianism in this way, is a practical religion within reach of every man and child, however poor his intelligence. It is almost completely lacking in dogma. The only dogma is contained in the first three words of the Bible, "In the beginning God created" (*beroshit bara elohim*): that is, that there is a single creative spirit behind all material things and all natural evolution. Knowledge of this Supreme Being comes from experience, from trust — *emanah*, faithfulness — not from any access of belief, which the Greeks call *pistis*, or from the recognition that something is true as the result of speculation or a moment of fancied revelation. Indeed, it is a remarkable experience for one like myself, who was brought up both on the Old Testament and at a later stage on Greek philosophy, to find how completely lacking the Hebrew Bible is in any form of dialectic. If you want theology, you must go to Plato or Neo-Platonists. The Bible rarely argues or reasons. It assumes, rather that the truth is accepted as a matter of experience and uses all the arts of rhetoric and emotional appeal to persuade people to live in the light of that truth. Yet one book, perhaps under the influence of Greek philosophy, is written in the form of a dramatic dialogue. Here the method used is that of litigation — and in the highest court of appeal. Job, the innocent plaintiff, arraigns the Almighty, and with magnificent invective curses "his day" and all the calamities that flesh is heir to. But the defense pursues a different tactic. Scorning the familiar arts of dialectic, it soars into a realm of universal values and by a series of tremendous and majestic assertions not only refutes the charges, but seems almost to reduce them to irrelevancy. "Where wast thou when I laid the foundations of the earth?" Even here there is no attempt at proof.

But though the supremacy of God is the central theme of the Hebrew scriptures, it must not be thought for a moment that Judaism belittles man or regards him as insignificant. On the contrary — and this is what needs to be conveyed to the modern child more urgently than anything else, by word as well as by deed — it teaches the limitless significance of every human being as (to use a phrase coined by a modern thinker, Martin Buber) "the unrepeatable experiment of God." It is a commonplace of modern psychological thought that the more industrialized and collectivized our society becomes, the greater the psychic dangers that beset the individual. A professor of education recently said that the great social problems that confront us can be explained by the fact that we do not know the name of our own postman. "This could not have happened in the old village society where every member was known to every other in terms of personality and no one could be a mere robot. But nowadays life has become industrialized and technological. We are caught up in a vast machine in which each one of us feels himself to be less than a cog. The machine could go on very well without us. Wherein, then, lies our personal significance?"

This is, surely, the unconscious basic question that the child is always putting to us and the one which society's builders today, who are so rarely taught of the Lord, find it the most difficult to answer. Here again it is our failure that has led to so much antisocial behavior on the part of young people who are "deprived" in the sense that they have never been given the chance of realizing their full richness and potentiality as created persons, thus examplifying the limitless creativity of their Creator. Take, for example, the sphere of family relations which provides one of the basic challenges of our time. The beauty and purity of Jewish home life have become proverbial and the subject does not need any special elaboration. What is not always recognized is that they spring from this basic doctrine of respect for human personality as created in the divine image. This is applied to the weakest and youngest members of the household who are all persons deserving honor in their own right. "Blessing enters the house only because of the wife," is a saying from the Talmud. Another is that when the little children went into captivity the *shechinah* (the presence of God) went with them. The divine city, according to Zechariah, "shall be full of boys and girls playing in the streets thereof."

This brings us to a second insight of Judaism which may have an important bearing on the issues raised by the modern child's spiritual hunger. The image of children playing in the streets — we must, I suppose, think of fields or playgrounds since the invention of the internal combustion engine — as well as that of conjugal relations raises the whole question of what we mean by the spiritual and material (organic) terms constantly regarded as antithetic and fundamentally in opposition to each other. This concept of antithesis arises from Hellenic sources and it led, as we know, to a constant debasement of the material things of this world and this earth. The Platonic myth of the cave and its shadows gives a wonderfully eerie picture of the unreal, distorted quality of terrestrial life as opposed to the ideal, spiritual life of reality, of the universal "idea." It led to the idea that the best we can do here and now is to prepare for escape to the world of the spirit through austerity and the practice of asceticism. As a modern Catholic theologian, Claude Tresmontant, has put it, to the Hellenic, particularly the Neo-Platonic school of thought, the physical world including man was a degradation of the One, so that existence in this world is an exile: "The body is a tomb; the soul's 'incorporation' a downfall. From this (according to Plato) we see in what direction we should strive: from here below to there above, the promptest possible escape."

To Hebrew philosophy, on the other hand, there was no contradiction in the universe. Since the one God created it, it bears the impress of his own nature: "He saw that it was good." The dichotomy between the material and the spiritual, between body and soul, therefore disappears. "The biblical world is a world in which the idea of matter does not occur," and this outlook seems to me fundamental to any consideration of the issue which is the subject of these lectures. For many of our moralists still turn in despair away from life, and certainly away from the warm religious life, and look for a panacea at one end of the scale in an economic or Marxist heaven, and at the other in some kind of spiritual stratosphere. What might be called the serenity of Judaism lies in its capacity to teach young people that they can completely satisfy their spiritual hunger in the so-called material world. It inspires man to work out his destiny in the world of fact and change and conflict that he knows, in the belief that he is a partner in the divine plan whose consummation depends, as far as man is concerned, on the goodness, vision, and courage that he displays during his mortal pilgrimmage. Of the hereafter, though Hebrew philosophy lays down unequivocably the principle of the soul's immortality, it can from the nature of things have little precise knowledge. The implications of such an outlook are immensely important when applied to the life of the child. It means that he can enjoy to the full, without any sense of guilt, the material blessings which are now so copiously within his reach. The considerations with regard to the limitations of such enjoyment, imposed by man's own authentic nature as one who plays a part in the total creative purpose, must be left for the moment because it is so important to emphasize that what we call the "good things of life" are also the gift of God. According to the rabbis, man need not refrain from enjoying the fragrance of the rose, the sexual act, the drinking of wine, and other bounties of nature. Rather, he must draw the fullest enjoyment from these and at the same time render thanks to their giver.

This teaching about the unitary pattern of life — that there is no fundamental dichotomy between the so-called spiritual and the material — has some very fruitful by-products where children are concerned. It helps them to be uninhibited in the best sense of that word, and removes the danger of their incurring, as they so often do in the modern world, a permanent unconscious sense of guilt or "guilt complex," as it is called, with all the mental disorders that arise from it. If the principle of *emunah*, an infinite trust in the world and in life, becomes part and parcel of the child's early experience, it will help him to satisfy his own ego and find personal significance in all the healthy and creative ways open to him. At the same time, when he attempts to find outlets for enjoyment and self-expression which are less healthy and less creative, if and when this is brought home to him he will not suffer any permanent mutilation of his

spirit or complete sense of failure, for he will know that
even in his aberration he is still the child of his Maker,
that he can never become what used to be called a lost
soul.

A second result of this peculiarly Hebraic view about
the nature of reality and consequent attitude towards
material things is especially emphasized in the sphere of
prayer. While the Hebrew prayer book abounds in en-
treaties to our heavenly Father for what may be called
the higher things of life — that he may endow us with a
portion of his own attributes, with grace, moral courage,
justice, compassion, and love — it does not scorn at the
same time to ask him for all kinds of legitimate material
benefits. To quote a few phrases from the modern Jewish
prayer book: "May the earth yield her increase," "Riches
and honor come of thee," "O lighten mine eyes lest I
sleep the sleep of death." This is the aspect of prayer
that quite naturally appeals to children and I cannot help
quoting the story of a little girl who knew, as children
instinctively do, on which side her bread was buttered.
One evening as she was saying her bed-time prayers in
front of her mother and grandmother, she concluded
in a very loud voice, "And please, God, will you give me
a motor car for my next birthday." Her mother looked
reproachfully at her and said, "You needn't shout so
loud, my dear; God isn't deaf." "No, I know, Mummie."
replied the child, "but Granny is." From the Hebraic
standpoint, there is nothing intrinsically amiss about
the child's approach, and the quiet assumption that a
gift from her grandmother is a gift from God is an altogether healthy one. Prayer brings to children the warm,
comforting experience that they are in a world that can
be relied upon and that cares for them.

But here it may be said that there is some danger of
spiritual complacency, a kind of positivism which accepts
things that happen because they happen. If we stop at
this point and make no kind of value judgment, it could

lead to an utterly false sense of security in the child's mind, with the most disastrous effects in his whole behavior and attitude to life. In answer to this let it be plainly stated, if it needs stating, that neither prophet nor rabbi, who were jointly responsible for the whole edifice of Judaism, ever failed to recognize the existence of evil and its devastating consequences. Far from being complacent about it, they concentrated much of their thought on the doctrine of the *yester tov* and the *yester ra,* the good and evil inclination which had been planted in men, and besought men with threat, objurgation, and entreaty to be on their guard against the latter with all its insidious wiles, its fatal capacity to lure them to their destruction. It is indeed sometimes said that the Talmud is obsessed with the sense of sin, a horror of *chillul hashem* (profanation of the Holy Name), of which there is a most detailed analysis sometimes carried (from our modern viewpoint) to the wildest lengths of exaggeration and absurdity. Yet the conflict between good and evil never reached metaphysical proportions. There was no contradiction at the heart of things. The same God "formed light, created darkness, made peace, and created evil." And man, who was formed in his image, could never stray outside the pale of his concern, of his responsibility. Man had, indeed, implanted within him the choice between good and evil, but even when he chose the latter there was always the opportunity of return (the Hebrew equivalent of repentance) through his own effort, and God was there to welcome him.

It is in this third category of its total insight that Judaism has its own special technique for dealing with the spiritual hunger of the modern child, as with that of every other human being. The term used for it is *halacha*: a way of life, literally the way which you walk. It derived from the ancient Pharisees, who, although much maligned in literature and current thought, were, in fact, the first to realize that, human nature being what it is, if resistance to the evil inclincation was to be effective and the practice of good cultivated, this could only be done through a sustained and constant discipline starting in the home with children when they were young and carried out through all the various occupations and pursuits of adult life.

It was the Pharisees who laid down the form by which life and its every act could be consecrated to God. They, more than any Roman, upheld the virtues of *mores ac instituta*, morals and rules, and of *haec disiplina nostra*, this our teaching. In their hands, religion became a practical and ennobling force. After the fall of the Temple, with no national framework to ensure continuity, it is not surprising that it was the rabbinic element, with its tremendous development in the early centuries of the Christian era, that enabled Judaism to survive among the scattered remnants of the people. It is still the mainstay of their religious life at the present day.

In this connection, Dr. Parkes has pointed to a piece of evidence which is often overlooked. As is well known, the gravest concern of the Hebrew prophets was the practice of idolatry. Their pages teem with denunciations of idol-makers and backsliders who worship the *baalim* and bow down to stock and stone. Indeed, a foreign queen, Jezebel, was able to introduce the dieties of her own country and almost destroy the worship of God in the Nothern Kingdom. By the time the New Testament was written, there is hardly a mention of idolatry or the worship of strange gods. The Pharisees and the rabbis had effectively applied the old principle, "These words shall be in thy heart, thou shalt teach them to thy children," "Thou shalt talk of them when thou sittest in thy house, when thou walkest by the way, when thou liest down and when thou risest up."

There is no time tonight to elaborate on this theme and to show how in a good Jewish home the children are prepared to resist the seductive worship of the many idols of our own age, but I may be forgiven, perhaps, for saying something about the Jewish Sabbath eve celebration because, according to Sir Basil Henriques, it is largely on account of this unique weekly event that there are proportionately so many fewer juvenile delinquents among the Jewish community in England than in the surrounding population.

The evening starts with the mother lighting the Sabbath candles as a symbol of joy and gladness at the approach of the day of rest. The prayer she utters runs as follows: "Lord of the Universe, I am about to perform the sacred duty of kindling the lights in honor of the Sabbath, even as it is written: 'And thou shalt call the Sabbath a delight, and the holy day of the Lord honorable.' And may the effect of my fulfilling this commandment be that the stream of abundant life and heavenly blessing flow in upon me and mine; that thou be gracious unto us and cause thy presence to dwell among us. Father of Mercy, O continue thy loving kindness unto me and unto my dear ones. Make me worthy (to rear my children that they) walk in the way of the righteous before thee, loyal to thy law and clinging to good deeds. Keep thou far from us all manner of shame, grief, and care; and grant that peace, light, and joy ever abide in our home. For with thee is the fountain of life; in thy light do we see light. Amen."

There follows the recital of certain prayers, hymns, and psalms, the most delightful of which has the refrain, "Come, my friend, to meet the bride: let us welcome the presence of the Sabbath." The Sabbath is figuratively regarded as a bride coming to her home, and in other sections of Jewish literature as a princess. Then there is the blessing of the children by the father in the familiar terms of the priestly blessing — "The Lord bless thee and keep thee," and so on. This is followed by the recital of Proverbs 10-31, "A woman of worth who can find? For her price is far above rubies," in honor of wife and mother. Finally before the evening meal, the *kiddush*, a sanctification ceremony over wine and bread.

The meal (a particularly good meal) ends with the singing of Psalm 126 — "When the Lord turned again the captivity of Zion, we were like unto that dream" — and the grace after meals which concludes with the words, "The Lord will give strength unto his people: the Lord will bless his people with peace." The rest of the evening is spent at home, in the family circle. There is no going out to parties or cinemas or theaters on this particular night in observant Jewish circles, nor is there much desire. This night is looked forward to throughout the week as a night of peace and joy and leisure, when work and week-day cares can be for a brief moment set aside.

This, then, is typical of the lived religion of practical Judais where there are always things for the children to do and see. It would take too long to describe the many other observances and ceremonies that make up the religious calendar, but one word may be said about the Day of Atonement when there is a twenty-four hour fast to give the opportunity to each individual to bare his soul before his Creator, confess his shortcomings, and ask for forgiveness and strength to face the battle of life more courageously in the future. Children are not required to fast until they are confirmed, generally at thirteen years of age. Would it surprise you to know how often they say at a younger age, "Please, Daddy, can I fast this year?"

Educationally speaking, there is a reliance on symbols, on visual aids, and on activity methods which will, it is to be hoped, more and more tend to dominate educational policy. At a recent conference, Mr. G. H. Bantock, a lecturer at Leicester University, advocated this type of education in terms which are extraordinarily applicable to the subject we are considering, the satisfaction of the child's spiritual hunger. "The common factor involved in all this is some return to the concentration on symbol and image rather than on intellectual processes — handwriting, painting, pottery, weaving, as well as the traditional wood and metal crafts, are what I have in mind; and the teddy boy uniform and the now popular coloured stockings worn by young people indicate something of the contemporary craving for colour in a drab world. But these things should be treated from the point of view of forming taste in relation to contemporary design, as well as from the technical standpoint. This, too, will link with the sort of domestic training that aids home building." These are words of wisdom and much in the Jewish religious training of children rests on this practical approach. For, as we have already been reminded in this series, religion, by and large, is caught, not taught.

There is a fourth and last insight of Judaism which bears so closely on the contemporary scene that I must not leave it unmentioned. It may be said by a critic of what I have said thus far that it all concerns the child belonging to one particular denomination. It may have wonderful results in his case, but what about the vast majority of the world's children who are never likely to come under Jewish religious influence? The answer is that there lies at the root of Jewish teaching a deep-seated spirit of tolerance and that it is always hoped that the ethical and social principles which form the staple of the Jewish ethos may, *mutatis mutandis*, the necessary changes being made, be exemplified in other religions and philosophies as well.

Recent history, especially that black page containing the story of Nazi Germany, has shown that man is particularly liable in a stage of uncertainty and insecurity to fall prey to the disease of intolerance. For this there are many causes — social, psychological, and economic — but what is certain is that it arises basically from man's egocentric tendencies which so magnify the importance of self as to leave no room for the respect of others. The Greeks call this *hubris* and it lay at the root of their conception of tragedy, though here it was the province of gods that was being encroached upon rather than the rights of mortals.

In this sphere of human relations, religion on the whole has an unhappy record. The bitterest wars have been waged, the most revolting cruelties perpetrated by those who claimed to possess the whole of divine truth and sought violently to compel others to accept their beliefs. What memories of persecution and torture are called to mind by the constant repetition of such words as infidel, heretic, inquisition, and damnation in the medieval history books!

Yet even here ancient Hebrew teaching has shown the way, and modern Judaism, with all the advantages of a long intervening apprenticeship in rabbinic humanism, has completed the evolutionary process. A tolerant pattern of behavior was first commended in such books as Jonah and Ruth and many stray Biblical injunctions, as, for instance, "Abhor not an Edomite" (Isreal's traditional foe), and "Love ye therefore the stranger" (i.e., the foreigner) "for ye were strangers in the land of Egypt." And this, in the old days, meant religious as well as racial tolerance.

This spirit was immensely strengthened by later rabbinal development and if there were any earlier symptoms of exclusiveness or spiritual pride, they tended to disappear through the humanistic teaching of the rabbis and medieval philosophers like Maimonides. Lacking any special soteriology or doctrine of salvation, Judaism was able to recognize the significance and values of other religious insights. "The righteous of all peoples have a place in the world to come." And this was only possible because the rabbis made no attempt to impose their discipline on other peoples. Active proselytizing disappeared soon after the first century of the Christian

era, and it became the established view that all who lived
a life in accordance with the moral law, first formulated
in the pre-Torah Noachic principles, would merit the
"kingdom to come." One rabbi even went so far as to
declare that "all who accept merely the Ten Commandments may be considered as accepting the whole Law."
It is this attitude of tolerance — even at the intellectual
level — that enables Judaism to throw fresh light on
one of the most baffling problems of our sorely distracted world. For ultimately it judges people not on
what they believe but on how they behave towards one
another. It would echo that superb Gandhian (almost
Chassidic) sentiment that, "A society's civilisation should
not be judged by its power over the forces of nature, nor
by the power of its literature and art, but by the gentle-
ness and kindness of its members towards all living
beings."

Young people today, and I think in every age, are disposed to be tolerant of groups other than their own,
but here again, their spiritual hunger remains unsatis-
fied. As Dr. Cyril Bibby says in his book *Race, Prejudice
and Education*, "From the very earliest days infants are
imbibing the implicit assumptions of the society in which
they live; and, if the social environment is one of racial
discrimination, it will be difficult indeed for a child to
grow up without taking it for granted that such a state
of affairs is part of the natural order of things."

To the present world rent by nationalism, claims of
racial superiority, and ideological conflict, modern
Judaism would reassert the principle of the dignity and
equality of all men as children of the universal father.
The most important verse in the Bible, thought Rabbi
ben Azzai, was, "This is the book of the generations of
man" — not of Jew or Gentile, of white, black, or yellow,
but of all men irrespective of their race, creed, or color.
It is the Hebrew counterpart of that pregnant Roman
line of Terence that used to be shouted across the Roman
theater: *"Homo sum; nihil humani a me alienum puto."*

"I am a human being and everything human has a claim on my sympathy." It represents an attitude that does not seek to obliterate differences, but pays homage to each individual soul as expressing in some measure its author's creative spirit.

This brings us to a final restatement of the proposition with which this paper started: If we are to satisfy the spiritual hunger of children and so help to create the good society of the future in this distracted world of ours, its builders must be taught of the Lord; and modern Judaism, with its special genius and historical experience, has four distinctive techniques to offer in the accomplishment of this task.

The first consists in an emphasis on practice rather than dogma or theory. At the root of Judaism lies the assumption that man is created with a purpose, that he is fulfilling that destiny only if he suits his conduct to that purpose, and that as a matter of experience and conviction the will of his Creator has been revealed to him. This insistence on practice, action, and deed appeals especially to children. In after years they may begin to doubt and grow skeptical; that is the time for them to study Greek philosophy or its modern counterparts. But when they are young they do not question that "it hath been shown thee, O man, what is good."

The second is its insistence on the unitary pattern of life, that there is no ultimate transcendental distinction between the natural, the psychic, and the spiritual; that the same creative spirit is responsible for the physical things we enjoy with our appetites and desires, as well as the nobler impulses of our minds and hearts. If this is accepted, there is less danger of a child suffering from a permanent sense of guilt or inferiority since he will realize that both his body and soul have a unique significance in the mind and purpose of the Creator.

Thirdly, as both the evil and good inclinations have been planted in him and man is liable to stray from his essential humanity, Judaism insists that a way of life or discipline is essential to him at his present stage of evolution. Through the practice of what is called *torah*, the stream of divine teaching, man may learn to control his evil desires and by a process of *imitatio dei* — imitation of God — pursue the life of goodness, charity, unselfishness, and love. Hence the constant reminders through prayer, ceremony, and observance in home and synagogue that every act of life should be consecrated to the service of God.

And fourthly, Judaism is deeply imbued with the spirit of tolerance so needed at the present time. Lacking any soteriological dogma, it judges men by their action and behavior rather than by what they believe; still less does it attach importance to their racial origin or the color of their skin. In this it would make a special appeal to young children who so often fail to understand the prejudices of their elders and naurally tend, if they are allowed, to take people as they come.

I would not, in conclusion, like to leave the impression that I think that modern Judaism, or indeed any one religion or philosophy, gives all the answers or can offer a panacea for the various ills from which our generation is suffering. Religious institutions are man-made, and however much they lay claim to divine inspirations they are liable, like other human beings, to drawbacks and limitations. But I would say that as a divine frame of reference, its healthy insistence on practice, and its optimistic belief in the ultimate perfectability of human beings through effort and discipline and adventure qualify it to cater for the spiritual hunger of both child and adult in a way that is sane, imaginative, and psychologically effective. To use the concluding phrase of the Jewish Sabbath morning service, it would help us all, in this challenging but terrifying world, to say and to feel, "*Adonay li velo yra.*" "The Lord is with me. I will not fear."

QUESTIONS

Q. At the end of the discussion last week, someone asked Rev. Bittleston whether he felt that in the family there are certain duties and responsibilities that fall to the father and others that should be reserved for the mother, or whether a certain mingling of duties — such as the father taking care of the baby's physical needs — might be appropriate. I would like to put this question again to Mr. Polack: How are the roles of the father and mother seen within the Jewish family?

Mr. Polack: Yes, this is a very interesting question. Perhaps it may be of interest to some of those present that, according to Jewish teaching and law, the child, in the case of a mixed marriage, follows the religion of the mother and not the religion of the father. And that, to some extent, answers the question. In the Jewish concept of family life, and in religious teaching and training, there are certain duties laid down for the mother and certain duties laid down for the father. They are, of course, complementary in a sense, and not antithetic. The mother, for instance, has all the duties which have to do with the domestic part of life; with provision of food, with sustenance, with the whole of the child's natural center of thought. The father is more concerned with the technical, educational side; the teaching of Hebrew, the teaching of prayer, the bringing of the child to the synagogue. He takes a greater part in the synagogue and the outward religious ceremonies. But when it comes to the general human challenge, there it is very difficult to draw any distinction with regard to functions. I would say that they should be shared.

Q. You say it is the father's duty to give the religious upbringing to the child. If so, what happens in the case of the mixed marriage, when the child takes the religion of the mother?

Mr. Polack: I would say that the theory of the child

taking the mother's religion rests on the fact that in the earlier stages it is the mother who says the prayers with the child and who gives even the early religious training. When intelligence begins to develop and the child grows up, the father takes over; but the spirit of religion permeates in the first years of life through the mother.

Q. It seems that this is the result of real tolerance, the belief we all share that there is only one God.

Mr. Polack: Yes, I doubt if in any good Jewish family any conflict between father and mother arises. There are plenty of conflicts between fathers and mothers about other things, but I think that in regard to the spiritual unbringing of the child, when both belong to the same faith, there is, as you say, the principle of tolerance which plays an extremely important part and allows mutual cooperation. The father recognizes that the mother has the vital role to play in the early years. For one thing, the father is not there; he is probably working.

Q. Even if the mother is not of the same faith?

Mr. Polack: There of course the child will be brought up in a different faith and the father would not then play any part; it would be difficult for him to play any part.

Q. Not even later?

Mr. Polack: I would say that where — as so often happens in Britain, for instance — the marriage is to a Christian, an Anglican, then the father probably becomes pretty lax. But occasionally both keep their own religion and the father would then, out of the spirit of tolerance, allow the mother to bring the child up in the Christian way. The father would continue his own loyalty to his own faith and synagogue, but he would not interfere with the child's upbringing except to join in when possible.

Q. Would it be a good idea for the father to take the child to synagogue and the mother to church on Sunday? After all, they are on different days.

Mr. Polack: I think that is rather a heavy meat for the child. You see, the problem in mixed marriages is that it is very confusing to a young child. Any great difference between father and mother is confusing, and it is especially confusing to a young child to see a different religious loyalty going on in his own family. In fact, it sometimes leads to very unhappy results. So I do not think that would be a good plan. I know in some families where there has been a mixed marriage that one of the children is brought up in one faith and one in the other. If the father takes one boy to the synagogue on the Sabbath, the mother takes the girl or another boy to church on Sunday. That I have known happen. And they had decided to let the children make up their own minds later on; but I do not think it is a happy arrangement myself.

Q. Are there many Jews who do not keep their religion, who are not observant?

Mr. Polack: Oh, yes, I am afraid that is true, as in all denominations. The Jewish people are susceptible to and influenced by the current agnosticism, scientific materialism, and humanism like anybody else, and therefore many of them have given up their Judaism. They are free human beings. I would say that the majority of them do not keep the full religious program, but they do keep a certain loyalty to their faith and to their group. They probably go to synagogue on New Year and the day of Atonement — the two most important days of the year — and they take their children to be confirmed in the synagogue, they marry there and so on. On the other hand, a significant minority do keep the discipline sincerely.

Q. The proportion of juvenile delinquents among Jews in this country is lower, I believe, than in any other community. You attributed that to the Sabbath, to the ritual of the Sabbath meal, but that is probably not practised by more than twenty percent of the total Jewish population in England. Yet somehow the effect

is there, even among those who do not do this practice;
so it seems to me there is still some secret up your
sleeve!

Mr. Polack: I would say that they are living on the
capital of the past — a certain moral quality or richness
has been handed down to Jewish children even when
the families have completely thrown the practical religion overboard. You see, certain traditions have come
into Jewish home life. The purity and sanctity of Jewish
home life have remained even when the actual observance, the ceremony, is no longer kept. I think I ought
to say also that the Jewish people as a group feel that
they have a priestly function to perform in the world.
They have always had this; they are joined together by
their history to some extent, by the feeling that they
have something specific to give to the total welfare of
mankind. This comes from a priestly, messianic, emotional outlook which is deeply within Jewish people,
even when they have given up the forms and ceremonies
of their religion. That is why you find so many of them
taking a leading part in all sorts of philanthropic movements. But I would say that the Friday evening ceremony
is actually observed by rather more than twenty percent.
It has lingered on, partly as a focus of family life. And for
those who have thrown overboard the whole tradition
of observances, there is still the atmosphere lingering
because their relatives — their sisters and their cousins
and their aunts and so on — are probably still of the
Jewish faith. Even if the parents have thrown over a great
many of their religious customs, they do bring the
children up in the faith to some extent. And therefore,
there is that indefinable ethos or atmosphere which per-
vades the Jewish home even if it is no longer a center of
practised Judaism. It is intangible, but I think it is there,
and it affects the children; and I think that is why they
retain, on the whole, a greater sense of the importance
of home and family life than most communities. I do not
want to exaggerate this, but I am told that this is so.

Q. Isn't it true that even though they may have thrown over the ritual, the part of the religion concerned with the education is still adhered to very strongly? I was very impressed by a statement made by two fellow naval officers; one was a chaplain in the Royal Navy — a Church of England chaplain — and the other was a Royal Navy Reserve officer. Both of them, in peace time, had worked in the East End — the R.N.V.R. officer as a policeman, and the chaplain as a curate to an East End church. Both of them remarked that in the poorest quarter of the East End, if you saw children who were well-dressed and slightly over-fed, you could always say that they were from Jewish parents; and if you saw the parents, you were shattered: They were in rags and going hungry. Whereas in a lot of other cases the money was spent on drink and other things rather than on the children.

Mr. Polack: I can well believe that because it is so deeply in the Jewish soul that children must be cared for and loved, and given a fair chance in this world. It may be partly due to the fact that they have always been a persecuted people, and persecuted groups tend, I suppose, to be more protective, tend to be warmer in their intimate life. I believe that the effect of persecution of the Jewish people has been to make them emphasize family life. It often makes them over-indulge children, as you said, but it certainly has kept them from the rather detached, if not cruel attitude of many parents which has led sometimes to serious deprivation. I think that is almost totally absent among Jewish parents.

Q. We seem to have turned the fourth commandment upside down from, "Honor thy father and thy mother" to "Honor thy son and daughter."

Mr. Polack: Yes, there is a lot in that. Jewish literature abounds in the attachment and love for children. I have put only a few quotations across, but if you study the Talmud, it is inherent.

Q. Is it not true that a Jew who ceases to observe tends to fall into agnosticism or humanism? Is there not some emotional factor?

Mr. Polack: The weakness of Judaism, from my point of view, is that it never quite comes to grip with the intellectual, or with the metaphysical puzzle which is inherent in the universe. There is no theology in Judaism. Theology means science about God, and for this one must go to philosophy of various kinds right through the ages, starting with Hellenism. And there are young Jewish intellectual people now who say that they cannot swallow this religion any longer. They have real skepticism, and they drift to some other belief, often scientific humanism. They do reject the theistic interpretation of life, which is inherent in Judaism.

Q. Are there no more esoteric forms of Judaism than the rabbinical teaching?

Mr. Polack: We are now learning a great deal more about the Dead Sea Scrolls. There were Essenic groups of Jewish people who became monastic, but Judaism through history has been largely free of that kind of mystic or monastic system. The emphasis is on the practical, on life as we know it; living in the family, bringing children into the world, marriage, and so on. Good deeds and the service of God are to be exemplified in the busy world of the city, in the marketplace, and the countryside. That is emphatic in rabbinic Judaism, and any earlier monastic tendencies disappeared. There is a literature called the Kabbala, or kabbalistic literature, which is a mystical literature. It has played its part, but on the whole the main stream of Judaism has been within the sphere of the practical, civic, and national life of the people amongst whom the Jews lived. You see the enormous effect of Jeremiah's advice to the Jewish exiles when they were taken captive — "Seek ye the peace" — again this word *shalom* — "Seek ye the peace or the welfare of the city whither I have caused ye to be carried

away captive, for in the peace thereof ye will find peace."
Good citizenship, you see, inculcated from very early
times. It is amazing for a scattered people, a people subjected to all kinds of persecution and a complete lack of
human rights right through the Middle Ages. It is amazing
to see to what extent they were loyal to the king and
country. It is interesting to read the prayer for the royal
family in the Jewish synagogue, or the American prayer
for the government, and so on. Loyalty to the established
government, wherever possible, is part and parcel of the
Jewish heritage. Whether this is always a good thing, I
do not know, but it is implicit in Jewish life and that
is why, on the whole, Jews have been good citizens
and have never retired into the life of the cloister, away
from the national or the practical civil scene.

Q.   There is one point I would like to make. In most of
the lectures up to now, there has been a general agreement that the attempt to teach religion to children can
only lead to confusion and possible loss of faith. Religious teaching, we have heard, must come later. When
one hears of the Jewish teaching of prayers and the
teaching of religion by the fathers, one gets the impression that there is plenty of religious teaching in
Judaism. Listening carefully to what you said, it seems
to me that you have really made this point clear: It is
a practice that is taught, not a doctrine or theory. I
would like to be sure that there is agreement on this
point, because it seems to be one of the things that is
coming out of this series of lectures: The attempt to
teach spiritual doctrines to children will only confuse
them and perhaps even destroy the faith that is in them.

Mr. Polack: Yes, I substantiate that entirely from the
Jewish religious point of view. The child starts with
seeing something done, really, and wonders what it is
all about. When the child sees his mother light a candle
and you say it is Sabbath, you make the day different.
You cannot explain the principle of rest once in seven
days at that stage. Long before you train the children's

minds in religion, you give them things to do and
see, and read them the Bible stories. They get a kind of
natural awe; I don't know why, but they do. It seems to
come just from what is seen. When they see the candle
and take part in the passing of the bread and wine, it is a
thrilling symbol for them. That is how religion is gradually caught — not taught, but caught.

Q. But you did say just then, "Long before you begin to
teach religion": At what stage is there actual teaching of
religion? Does that begin after confirmation, or is it not
really like that at all?

Mr. Polack: No, I would say that children go to classes
at a much younger age than that. They may start at six
or seven to go to religious classes connected with the
synagogue, or their parents may start to teach them. But
here again, it is the teaching of what? It is teaching the
literature of the Bible stories. You may think that this
is a complication, but owing to tradition, sentiment,
and emotion much of the Jewish religious language is
still the old Hebrew, which is the language of the Bible.
At a very early age, this is a new language for children.
They are thrilled with the picture books which teach
them the Hebrew alphabet, and they get excited about
the new language. It is in this kind of way that they
are prepared to go to the synagogue. Jewish children
ask if they can come and see the scrolls; it is a great
thing to see. I expect some of you have seen these in
the synagogues; there are the most beautiful scrolls in
the Ark, which are taken out and chanted from. The
children also learn hymns, just as Christian children do,
and take part in a great many other ceremonies. The fact
that during one week in the year only unleavened bread
is eaten in an observant Jewish home has a dramatic
effect on the child's mind; so the religion is "caught"
through that kind of symbolism.

Q. It can only be "caught" from someone who has it?

Mr. Polack: Yes, that is the key to the whole problem
we are facing.

Q. Do you see any way of formulating your four basic points about the Jewish family life in a way which could be of help to non-Jewish parents who are concerned with this problem of the spiritual hunger of the child? Do you feel that some element could be taken from this which would not distort their own life or distort the Jewish teaching?

Mr. Polack: Yes, there are several. Literature is the best way. There are a number of books dealing with Jewish heritage, explaining what we can all derive from Jewish teaching, what constructive elements of Judaism we can apply to general social problems, and so on. There are frequently demands from ordinary schools and Sunday schools for literature about the Jewish point of view. That is the best way, I think, to do it. The Council to which I belong — the Council of Christians and Jews, which was founded by William Temple — supplies a number of speakers, both Christian and Jewish, who go around to schools, colleges, training colleges, church groups, rotary clubs, and other bodies and explain the basis of Judaism.

Q. In reading the Old Testament, I get the impression that the Jewish religion had teachers and rabbis who had young boys under them, such as the infant Samuel. It must have made a great impact on these children, to grow up knowing the Scriptures. Is this still done?

Mr. Polack: I think we must be careful about drawing evidence from the Old Testament about the rabbinic way of life, because the rabbinic movement did not start until fairly late, well after the Restoration. So what you read about in the Book of Samuel is a priestly function, not a rabbinic function — to wait on the High Priest and so on. But I would say that young children did go to rabbinic schools at a very early age; that is how Judaism was kept alive. You hear the story of a child of six or so who was considered too young to attend the school, and they found him listening on the window-

sill the next morning, absolutely frozen because he was
so terribly enthusiastic and inspired by what he had
heard. It is quite true, the rabbi does take a special
interest in young children, and in a country like England
you will find that every synagogue has its teachers, its
rabbis, who pay very special attention to the training
of the child. In fact, in some parts of London they go
to what is called Cheder three nights a week after school
hours; even very young children, going to primary
schools, go to the rabbinic talmudical school after the
school period is over and are brought up in a very intensive form of Judaism. Sometimes parents complain that
it is too much. The Jewish community life is faced with
the problem that, whereas in the past, Judaism could in-
form the whole of life, now tremendous influences are
brought to bear on parents to make their children well-
educated in the total sense of the word. This means a
great deal of application to all sorts of subjects — scientific subjects of all kinds, technological subjects of all
kinds. They have got to fit into modern society, and
this makes it more difficult for the purely rabbinical,
spiritual Jewish influence to be brought to bear on the
child.

Q. It is ideal to be able to give the young child this
real teaching?

Mr. Polack: Yes, there is no contradiction, really, between secular education and religious education in
the Jewish traditional ethos, but the Jewish religion
grew up at a time when life was not so complicated.
What Jewish teachers feel now is that we must retain
this extremely valuable thing which is at the root of
human conduct, but it is a terrible fight to find time
for the spiritual techniques of Jewish religious training
when the children have so many demands on their
time. The state, you see, comes into it. You have got
to go to school, you cannot take the children and put
them in a rabbinic school all day.

Lecture 7

Buddhist Ideals and Modern Education

Maung Ji, M.A.

Common sense is a scarce commodity in our civilization, and many of us find that it is beyond our reach to
acquire it. This rare commodity is particularly wanting in
handling the young in our restless age. Our concept of
education for the young, and even for the old, is rather
farfetched and too difficult for practical application in
training children and parents alike. It is, therefore, necessary for us not to be a prisoner of a particular group of
ideas in education, but to learn from personal experience
and research in the likes and dislikes of children. This
seemingly simply analysis can help us to study the
emotional knots in children and to untie them for their
self-expression. We are often impatient with them with
no thought of harming them. But this lack of harmony
between children and parents often drives fear and
hate into the young minds to the detriment of their
healthy growth — physically, emotionally, and mentally.

Children, as a rule, are more awake bodily than we are
and they can therefore observe what their elders are
doing unnoticed by the elders themselves. They are,
however, less awake emotionally and mentally and are
living almost on the surface of life. Their emotions are
unreliable and their thinking power devoid of selective

ability. Physical care is therefore the first step for molding the young for acquiring suitable emotional, mental, and spiritual backgrounds for their education. We have to face our children in a humane way. Parents and teachers cannot bring up those under their care without making a few sacrifices and undergoing hardships in their relationship with the young.

A child has yet to experience the vicissitudes of life. He is molding his future not by thinking what his present deeds will accumulate for him in the future, but merely by living in the present with no knowledge of yesterday and tomorrow. He is unaware of intentions as we are accustomed to think of them in ethics and philosophy. His actions give him the sensation of the moment. Some of them please him and others displease him, and according to the nature of his experience he reveals his emotional tensions. He laughs. He cries. He alternates them according to his various moods. He lives in a small world of his own, a world in which moods play a greater part than facts of life. He is very sensitive emotionally and responds without any mental understanding to his immediate environment.

The child thus grows from day to day, gradually enlarging his emotional nature by the process of self-assertion of his likes and dislikes on which he builds, in due course, his individuality. In the earlier stages of his evolution, he thinks with the help of his emotions, often hampered by incomplete decisions and unrealized wishes. He is, truly speaking, feeling his way for growing more freely in the physical world than in the sphere of thought and emotion. His perception is little connected with memory and is therefore devoid of the sense of causality.

Physical environments will slowly shape the child according to the efforts of those who live with and near him. A winding and unwinding process goes on all the time in the inner life of the child, emotionally and mentally. Examples create a deeper and better impression on the child than precepts. Common sense is essential in handling a child. It is indeed the master key which can help us to unlock the potential powers both for good and bad in a child at home and at school. We should try not to forget our own childhood. We should remember that the fruit can bear flower only by the sacrifice of itself. Thus our sympathy for the child helps him to grow in happiness and to take his proper place in life.

Education for the young has always been a problem. It will not cease to be a problem as long as we live among our fellow men. Living creatures other than human beings have, in their own way, problems related to collective living and thinking and training themselves to possess herd mentality for safety and survivial in the unprotected, wild, jungle life. We will not, however, teach our children to acquire herd mentality, but we can help them to become social creatures capable of making sacrifices for the benefit of all in the family.

Personally, I would be quite satisfied with the normal growth of a child, and with a normal education. His body and mind are linked by his emotional nature, and he will in due time grow out of his narrow life by our help and understanding as a good friend giving to another friend. A child, like grown-up people, dislikes restrictions and discipline, but he appreciates a teacher who shares his joys and sorrows as a true companion in his dream land.

While I admit that a child has spiritual possibilities, we must not forget the fact that he will perish if he is neglected and underfed. Even the genius in him cannot live and function without a personality for enriching our civilization. His growth can be hindered or enhanced by us. He depends entirely upon us for his physical and emotional needs. In the realization of this duty towards the child, we can help him to unfold his spiritual nature.

My education has been rather cosmopolitan in its nature and concept, unbounded by geographical frontiers and man-made nationalism. I was born in Rangoon,

Burma sixty years ago, a country in which classless society exists, with no rigid practices of caste system to restrict the spiritual democracy of Buddhism. This living faith has been handed down from one generation to another for helping people of Burma to live in peace and for practising the Law of Righteousness of the Buddha.

My early years of childhood were spent with my parents in an atmosphere of happiness and simplicity based on the Buddhist way of life. For I was taught to say in Pali: "All that we are is the result of what we have thought: it is founded on our thoughts and made up of our thoughts. If a man speak or act with a good thought, happiness follows him like a shadow that never leaves him."

Thus did I start my adventure in search of spiritual experience, unchanged and changeless by time, in the Buddhist Middle Way for physical and spiritual harmony of man. I had the opportunity of meeting, at the age of ten, two leaders of the Theosophical Society in Rangoon: Mrs. Annie Besant and Bishop Leadbeater. I was allowed by my parents to go to India with them for my education and spiritual training at the headquarters of the Theosophical Society at Adyar, Madras. I had a happy childhood in the company of men and women of all races and religions in an atmosphere of friendliness and good will to all men.

In due course, I was sent to the Theosophical School at Benares in Northern India by Mrs. Annie Besant, under the care and guardianship of Mr. N. Sri Ram, who is now the International President of the Theosophical Society. The Theosophical School was a model school, based on the concept that a child, being a spiritual entity, could be helped to unfold himself with the help and unselfishness of teachers. This was really true from personal experience of my teachers, for their love and kindness changed me and brought stability in my life. Their method now helps me for solving the child's complicated mental troubles in this restless civilization.

Education is an endless process in the life of a man, starting from the cradle and ending only in the grave. School education is a first step to that end, and a man must ascend many a step before life's doors close upon him.

My university education was in a Theosophical College near Madras in South India. Mr. Jinarajadasa, who became the International President of the Theosophical Society after Mrs. Besant's death, played an important role in my university education. He was a Buddhist from Ceylon. His insight into man's mental nature was based on the practice of the Master's teachings in his own life: "You yourself must make the effort. Buddhas only point the way. Those who have entered the path and who meditate will be free from the fetter of illusion." Truly this is the way to acquire the Quiet Mind that is not afraid of facing emergency and despair, for "within the mind there is a Buddha, and that Buddha within is the real Buddha. If Buddha is not to be sought within the mind, where shall we find the real Buddha? Doubt not that a Buddha is within the mind, apart from which nothing can exist."

My education was still unfinished in 1920 when I was already a young man of twenty years old. Cambridge and legal training at the Middle Temple in London had played their part in helping me to acquire a sense of objectivity in life. Knowledge is a good companion, but it cannot take a man far in his quest for the truth, for only by living the Law can a man gain wisdom. There are, therefore, not many wise men in our civilization. However, we need not be depressed because our present system of education cannot produce prophets and seers for uniting man and man, and nation and nation in an organic growth of human society. Our happiness does not rest on the presence of the wise in our midst, but on our rational approach to the problems which beset us in our daily life. This attitude is essential if we are to make use of scientific discoveries for the benefit of mankind. We have made life on our own patterns, on our likes and dislikes. Education must now unmake our dislikes for acheiving international cooperation to save this fear-stricken mankind from being destroyed by our own hands. I am always happy to take stock of my life and be with Mahatma Gandhi, poet Rabindranath Tagore, and Sri Aurobindo once again in my mind. It was Mrs. Besant who introduced me to them for spiritual experience and growth. Mahatma Gandhi had advised me to live with and work for the poor, for to the Mahatma an intellectual sympathy was of no help whatsoever to the poor. Hunger and ill-health haunted them without respite until death overtook them. They wanted food. They wanted to live. They did not want advice on education for escaping from their wretched poverty. I have had my moments of despair and utter darkness in the early years of our struggle for political independence, but I am able to say now that my faith in Mahatma Gandhi ultimately conquered them. Poet Rabindranath Tagore and Sri Aurobindo were to me the core and essence of inward peace which was the outcome of their victory over hate and greed. They were the beings that stood in the center of their aspirations as masters of all times.

I am a mixture of the East and the West in my education. I have no doubt in my mind that I have greatly benefited from this mixed education and from my association with our leaders. They were pillars of strength to me in my weak moments and Light Divine in my darkest hours. For the purpose of education is to learn to respect not only saints and prophets, but all living creatures as well.

It is in this spirit that I have offered to you all a few suggestions for educating your children, for they are to you a source of joy as well as responsibility for helping them to become good men and women in the years to come. And I now wish you all happiness and success in educating your children.

QUESTIONS

Q. How did you spend your first ten years before you were with Mrs. Besant? Were you alone, or were you in a family?

Mr. Maung Maung Ji: I lived with my family. My parents were Buddhists. I had the desire of becoming a monk because I was and am very sensitive to pain and suffering of all living creatures.

Q. Were you a big family?

Mr. Maung Ji: We were eight in all — three brothers and five sisters — and were a very happy family.

Q. Is it the Buddhist doctrine that when a child is born, the personality is already there, and this will develop and you cannot change it by anything from outside?

Mr. Maung Maung Ji: A child is born with his own personality and its essential nature cannot be changed. He has brought with him his **past parami,** as it is known in Buddhist psychology: an accumulated experience of his past lives.

Q. Are there two parts, then; one the spiritual part which cannot be changed, and also all the accumulated habits which to some extent can be changed?

Mr. Maung Maung Ji: We cannot wipe out a child's spiritual nature and accumulated habits altogether. These will force themselves in varying degrees in the education of a child. This is where our help and understanding of a child is important.

Q. I have heard about the habits which were inculcated by Mrs. Besant and Bishop Leadbeater, such as great tidiness and so on. Do you think that this kind of discipline was good?

Mr. Maung Maung Ji: I do think that tidiness is a very good habit to be instilled in a child as well as in a grown-up person. Tidiness in thought, work, and deed is the first step for gaining harmony within a man. I have, of course, greatly benefited from the training I have had under Mrs.

Besant's guidance. She had helped me at the start of the journey — a long and perilous journey indeed — with her knowledge and wisdom, but I can only get to the end by my own efforts and self-discipline.

Q. Mario Montessori said at one of the previous lectures that even if there is no God, it would still be necessary to invent God for the sake of the child. What would you say to that?

Mr. Maung Maung Ji: The child will invent his own God. We cannot stop that. I certainly think that the child finds joy in inventing his own God. We must remember that none of us can think in the abstract, and what we call thinking is nothing but mental conversation in which we are arranging and rearranging ideas and information we have collected by sense perception. Man therefore makes God in his image of the best type, to which he gives divine attributes for his own satisfaction.

Lecture 8

The Subud Approach

J.G. Bennett

It is sometimes easier to use a picture than to give
explanations, and therefore I shall start with a picture
that will illustrate what I am going to say about the
spiritual hunger of children, and what contribution can
come towards satisfying that hunger from the new
spiritual movement called Subud.

Picture a young man sent far from his own country
to fulfill a task, and let us say there is a great difference
between the place he comes from and the one he goes
to. For example, it might be a thousand years ago,
when Baghdad was the most magnificent city of the
world and the Caliph Haroun-al-rashid the greatest of
rulers. There is a country far away in the north where
the people are called Saxons, and the Caliph decides
to send the young man from Baghdad to this far country
to find out how people live there, and how these Saxons
can learn something about all the new discoveries made
by the Arabs.

The young man starts off on the journey and eventually, with great perils, reaches England. The climate
is altogether different from Baghdad, where it is never
cold, and he has to wear quite different clothes, eat
quite different food, he is unable to speak with the

inhabitants. He has to start by learning how to keep alive, and then to learn the language. Until he has done all this, he cannot even begin to do the task for which he was sent. Now suppose — as he is learning all these things and adapting himself to this quite different way of life, with the change of the seasons and all the charm of the northern climate — he begins to forget all about the country from which he came. He marries a Saxon girl and settles down in this country, unaware that one day he will be called back, and that the Caliph will say: "Well, what have you done with this mission on which you were sent?"

This, as you know, is a favorite way of describing the coming of the spirit of man into this world, and the real significance of our life on the earth. It serves to suggest that our life here is not for this earth itself, but for a purpose that is beyond the earth and is connected with both the place from which we came and the place to which we shall return after our stay here. The picture is very much less drastic than the reality. To go from Baghdad to England is nothing compared with the process of birth of a child, the entry of the human self into the earthly life. This requires not only different clothes and a different language but even a different body that enables us to live here on the earth. Through that body, we must accustom ourselves to earthly life and, eventually, to accomplish a task that we have already forgotten.

The first assumption that I have to make is that we live here on this earth to accomplish something. We do not live here on this earth just to pass so many years and then die, nor do we live on this earth just to feed this body, satisfy its desires, educate this mind, satisfy its curiosity, and so on. I shall ask you to assume that we are here to use this body and this mind for the fulfillment of some task. I say this is an assumption or a hypothesis because there is no evidence to which we can point and say, "There is the sign, the proof, that we are here in that kind of capacity, that we are messengers, people sent to do something, and having done it, to return." The realization that this really is the true situation of our life on earth only comes after certain things happen to us. And it is about those things that I am going to try to speak tonight.

Now to come back to the analogy of the messenger who is sent to another country. The first thing is that he has to live under quite new environmental conditions and to communicate with people who are completely strange to him. It is the same with the child. The child that is born enters a strange country, puts on strange clothes — that is, this earthly body of ours — and has to communicate with strange people. They are strange because they have bodies different from which the spirit, or essence, or as I would also call it, the "potential soul," lived before birth. It is an inevitable and necessary part of our life on the earth that there should be a period set aside for acclimitization to the new conditions. That period is childhood and youth, or what we call the "preparatory age" during which the main need of the new being is to learn to live successfully here on this earth, to cope with the physical and psychic needs of earthly life. But this should not be done in such a way as to produce a complete forgetfulness of whence we came, and whither we shall return, and the reason for our presence here.

Awareness of the whence and the whither and why, and the acceptance of it and the living with it, is the spiritual life of man. This, as I understand it, is the true meaning of the word worship. Worship is the condition in which we remember and are conscious of what is really worthwhile, the reason and purpose of our existence. The state of remembering this is the state of remembering God. It is not necessary for us to have any specific picture of what this means. I shall speak this evening about Subud, which does not depend upon any particular picture. For example, it does not require any particular form of belief as to the nature of God, or the relations between man and God. It is enough that we assume that there is such a relationship and that it has, somehow or other, a quality that can be pictured in the way that I have described. We should picture ourselves as having come from God and returning to God. This does not mean that we can make for ourselves any picture of what this heavenly home, from which we came and to which we shall return, is really like, because we are in an even harder position than the young man who came from Baghdad and has become so engrossed in his English life that he has quite forgotton the Tigris and what palm trees look like.

If we now apply all this to our problem as parents and teachers, it should help us to see how our problem really divides into two parts: one is to acclimatize the new human being in this earthly environment, and the other is not to drive the child into complete forgetfulness of his origins and his goal. This means that we have a certain external responsibility; that is, what we call education — and that is really outside the scope of these lectures as I understand it. We have to remember that education is a very complex process involving many sides of our nature. There is one part of education that concerns the bodily life, the use of the bodily powers and functions; there is another part that concerns the different phases of the psychic life — the instincts, the emotions, the intelligence, the power of thought, imagination, the aesthetic capacity, and so on. All these form a group of closely interrelated powers that are necessary for our life on the earth, and a complete and satisfying system of education will take care of these in a balanced way.

That is only one side of the picture; the other side concerns the purpose which education is to serve. Why are we learning to adapt ourselves to this earthly life and to develop the powers that are latent in this body and this psyche with which we have been furnished? The questions "why," and "what is the purpose and end of it all," cannot be studied in the same way as earthly problems. What I am saying may seem to you quite arbitrary. You may say, "If you can teach other things, why can you not teach this?" Why can this not be conveyed in the same way as the knowledge of geography or history, of things that are remote from us in space, or events that are distinct from us in time?" The reason for that is that this reality from which the answers to "why" and "whither" will come is completely different in nature from the reality of this world, the reality that can be perceived through the senses. If we attempt to convey some notion of this other reality in the same terms as we convey notions about geography and history and the physical world − or even about the psyche of man − we falsify it and in effect suggest to the child that it is not really different from the reality of the senses. For example, if we speak about a celestial city, it conveys the impression of something like an earthly city. It is just at that point that the analogy between the messenger sent from Baghdad and the journey of the human spirit breaks down. We do not come from another city, more magnificent, with different conditions of existence and perhaps much greater and higher culture, but from an entirely different mode of existence, an entirely different condition of consciousness. So different that it defies description in any language that can be derived from the senses.

That is why I myself am convinced that attempts to arouse by means of description − by means of what is called religious teaching − an idea of the why of our existence so often results either in its being brought down to the level of everything else, or else in skepticism. This is the fate of most attempts to deal with spiritual problems in bodily or psychic terms.

Therefore, some quite different procedure is required, and I want to speak about that before I speak about the way in which the spiritual reality is to be kept alive. The one part of the picture which I drew for you which really must be the basis for our talking about this is that there is something in man which comes from an altogether different source than the terrestrial part of his existence. In other words, there is something in man which is not of the same nature as the earth. That something, which I shall just call the spirit of man, cannot have any contact with the earth unless there is some link between the two; and the link between the two is what we call the psyche, or the soul. I spoke in the first lecture about the hunger, or need, of the psyche. This psyche requires a material instrument; that is, this physical body with its nervous system.

We can scarcely hope to understand our problem unless we think of man as composed of three parts: a bodily, or somatic part; a mental, or psychic part; and a spiritual, or pneumatic part. The first of these is the result of the union of the father and the mother, and it carries with it all the hereditary elements that are brought into this new life. It is as if this messenger arriving in this new country has to receive a second-hand suit of clothes — and it has all the various defects an old suit of clothes would have. This is what we received from our parents, and that is what we transmit to our children: a certain organism carrying with it very much that has been tainted by ourselves, by our parents, by our ancestry in general. The same is also true for the whole psychic elements that have arisen out of the past ex-nature comes out of a pool, or reserve of psychic existence that is common to the human race. This has been called the "collective unconscious" by Jung and others. I am sure there is some foundation for the idea that we draw the material of our psychic nature from the general pool of human experience. A part comes rather directly from our parents; part, it may be, from some previous lives of our own; but in general, the human psyche is a compound thing that is the result of the past experiences of mankind — including our own, perhaps, in some way or another.

The reason we have to look at it that way is that it brings us before a very serious aspect of life on the earth. When we enter this earth and are provided with an instrument for earthly life, this instrument is itself defective. It carries itself somatically — in the physical body — the hereditary somatic elements, the genetic elements as they are called. It also carries the various psychic elements that have arisen out of the past experiences of all mankind, of our own parents and ancestors, and may, as I said (I might even say probably), carry past experiences that are somehow directly associated with ourselves. Now the soma and the psyche are the instruments with which spirit is provided to perform the task that it has come to the earth to perform. This introduces a factor that stands between the preparation for earthly life and the awareness of the nature of our task. We are unaware of our task, not simply because we forget why we have come to the earth, but also because the instruments with which we are living on the earth are themselves so closely connected with earthly existence, and particularly the past experience of mankind, that they cannot help us to remember. The problem with children, therefore, is not merely one of preparing their instruments so that they will be adequate for life on the earth, but also of purifying these instruments, of eliminating from them the defects which prevent them from serving their real purpose.

This, then, brings three distinct elements into our preparation for life on the earth. The first is the development of this body and the development of the natural powers latent in it. The second is the rectification of the inherited defects, which includes the universal defects common to the whole human race. The third is connected with the sense and aim of our existence upon earth, and corresponds to what I called the "memory of the task which we are sent to perform." It so happens that the third of these requirements cannot be met directly, for it depends mainly upon how the second is satisfied. Children's spiritual hunger really comes from the feeling that they are losing or have lost something. Mario Montessori, in his lecture, said that a child is not spiritually hungry because it is itself wholly spiritual; but he went on to say that we must not deprive children of the spiritual food they need. This apparent contradiction conceals a deep truth. In one sense, the child already has what he needs, because he brought it with him. In another sense, he is deprived of it because he has entered an earthly body and has become subject to the conditions of earthly life. This two-fold truth is the secret of understanding the child, and is also the secret of understanding ourselves, as human beings.

Before I go further, I must say a little about Subud for the benefit of those of you who know nothing about it. Subud is a movement that has only appeared in this country in the last five years, and which has its origin in the Far East. It is of special interest in our time because it does not call for any specific form of belief beyond the general attitude that we look for a purpose and significance for our lives in relation to a Divine Purpose and a Divine Significance. Everyone is free to interpret this purpose according to their own private beliefs and customs. This means that Subud is not something which has any teaching or doctrine of its own, but it is — I would call it — a spiritual method, or an action. As I have verified by my own experience over the last years, it is an action which does not reach us from the outside in the way that we learn by being told, or by imitating other people, or by reading, or from our experiences. It comes, on the contrary, from within ourselves and works through that spiritual part of our nature of which I have been speaking. It acts through all the different levels of our own nature, starting from the physical body — the soma, the organism — to the different parts of the psyche, the instincts, the feelings, the intellectual powers, the imagination, and so on. It works as if there were a renewal of the contact with the Source from which we came. With that comes a flow of life, similar to the flow of life by which a child is conceived, develops, and is born and grows in the world. Therefore, it is sometimes called a contact with the Universal Force of Life.

The action of this contact sets in motion a flow of life energy which renews the different parts of the body and the psyche, and restores them to near the true human condition. To put it in terms of the analogy I gave at the beginning, I would say that the messenger who comes to do a particular task acquires reliable instruments, the right sort of clothes, the right sort of food, the right understanding of the language of the country to which he has come, and also, with it all, a constant remembrance of the reason for his coming. He will be able to remember just because his instruments are in good order, and he therefore is not constantly frustrated and harassed by the failure of his instruments to provide him with what he needs.

Translating that back into the language of the three parts of man, one can say that what Subud proposes to man is an action that renews the bodily functioning and the different parts of the psychic functioning by contact with a vital force, and at the same time awakens the inner conscience, or inner consciousness, that enables man to see for himself, from within himself, why he is on the earth and what his life really means. He sees it not simply as a partial existence on the earth, but as a complete life, including the life from whence he came and the life to which he will go.

That is what Subud proposes — I do not like to say

"claims" — and I only need to say enough to enable me to go on with the description of the way in which Subud helps the spiritual needs of our children to be satisfied. You will understand that I am not giving a lecture about Subud, but trying to say something about this particular approach to the problem of satisfying the needs of children.

I think you will agree that a great deal of the disturbance of the psyche — and with it, also of the physical life of people at the present time — comes from the fact that they are not clear why they are here and what is the real significance of life on earth. Therefore, if some light can be thrown on this in such a way that a person can see for himself why he lives and where he is going, many of the tensions and troubles of earthly life will either disappear or be very, very much diminished.

How is it possible for parents and teachers and other people who have contact with children to do anything useful about this? I think, first of all, it is important for us to recognize that we are confronted with three distinct problems. The first can be solved by what we could call straight education, straightforward preparation of the instruments for life. That is a matter of technique. Techniques of education are developing, although they are still very inadequate for the optimum development of the natural powers. We are still a long way from a satisfactory educational procedure, but this is something that can be found by the scientific methods of observation, experimentation, and hypothesis. There is every reason to suppose that our educational procedures will make progress as time goes on.

The second problem is to deal with the defects. This is not by any means so simple as the first. It is not to be dealt with by the same sort of technique as what I call straight education; the straightforward development of the natural powers. It very often can happen that if one tries to remove a defect of character by some outward procedure, one simply drives it underground and it produces something worse. These are the well-known psychic effects of wrong handling of children by all kinds of pressures that are put on them to deal with various psychic defects. But this does not mean that this can be left alone. We must not make the mistake of thinking that as long as we take care of just the first egoism because he is putting in front of himself a Value, themselves. That might be true if there were no inherited defects in the psyche, in which case the psyche would develop quite naturally alongside with the body and its powers. But that is not the situation. It is really most necessary for everyone of us who has this question at heart to accept as a reality of human life on the earth that all of us carry defects, not only hereditary, but as a general condition of defectiveness. In religious terms, this is called *sinfulness,* but it is not necessary to express this in religious terms. We can express it simply in terms of the transmitted psychic defects of the human race and speak of it in purely psychological terms. It is very probable that we can find one single word that sums up the totality of these psychic defects — however varied they might be — and that one word is probably *egoism,* or self love. I might even have used the word self-worship, because this really means treating oneself as if one were worth more than anything else. May I say here that I speak about the common defects of our human nature. If I tried to make a full analysis of the psychic defects of mankind, we should find that no one word will convey the true nature of our trouble. I might have described it as a state of illusion, or delusion, or a state of imagining that things are quite different from what they really are, or I could have spoken of "original sin," but let us use the word egoism, which comes pretty near the truth.

This condition cannot be dealt with by the action of another psyche that is also tainted with the same defect; we cannot deal with the egoism of other people when we

are also tainted and filled with the same. It seems that
the only way in which egoism in children can be to some
extent alleviated is that the parents and those surrounding the children deal with their own egoism. This
has been referred to in several of the earlier lectures,
and I think it is one of the central points for a common
understanding of our problem. We cannot teach children
how to be good, we cannot teach children about egoism
and altruism, these can only be theories for them. What
we can do is convey to children that it is right and normal
for man not to be obsessed by himself and by not being
obsessed with ourselves. There is a lot to be said about
this, but I think you will understand what I mean without it being necessary for me to elaborate. It can be said,
in general, that insofar as the problem of psychic defects
is concerned, the only solution lies in those who deal
with children insofar as they are prepared to deal with
themselves. Certainly it would be absurd to propose that
none of us should have children until we were free from
egoism and other psychic defects, or that none of us
could become teachers until we are free from those
defects. The world would soon be depopulated and there
would be no schools. It seems to be true — and this is
very fortunate for mankind — that it is not really necessary that we should have arrived at a state of freedom
from psychic defects, but that we should have a genuine
wish to be free. The genuine acceptance of the burden we
place upon children by our own defects, and a wish to be
free from them, is the secret of helping them. That in
itself is enough to make a prodigious difference to the
whole feeling of the child about life, to its confidence in
this world, and also to its confidence that there is truly
a meaning in its existence. Whereas if, on the contrary,
parents and other people who deal with children try to
hide their own defects and to pretend that the ordinary
human being is free from defects, this will only cause
complete bewilderment, and probably revolt, and the

very opposite of what is hoped for from the children. I
have observed with children the remarkable positive
response that is always made to older people who do not
disguise the fact that both they as individuals, and the
rest of mankind, are defective. Distress and loss of confidence is caused when there is any kind of posing as
perfect or better, as if this somehow would give the
child confidence in grown-up people because they
pretend to be what they ought to be.

I say all that in passing, because it is not the whole
story. I must now speak about the third, that is, the
truly spiritual problem. What is it that we can do in
front of children, so that they will grow up with a sense
of a meaning of their lives, a confidence that the purpose
of their lives goes beyond this earthly existence and
therefore will enable them to live their lives quite differently? I am sure, first of all, that it is not in what we say
to children, it is not even the way in which we behave
towards children — that is, what I have been saying just
now, about the psychic problem. It is necessary that we
ourselves should begin to be aware of this reality in ourselves. This is not something that we can achieve unless
we receive help from a spiritual source.

Let us come back to what I have said about Subud, as
it will help you to see why particular advice is given to
parents who follow this practice of Subud — both by Pak
Subuh, the founder of the method, and by those who
have considerable experience of it. Their advice is that
you should not attempt to *teach* your children anything
about spiritual realities; but devote yourselves, as far as
possible, to the worship of God. From that worship of
yours there will remain in the child a contact with
Reality, and when he reaches the age at which he is able
to deal with the problems of outward life on the earth, he
will not have forgotten this inward truth.

I must say how I understand the phrase "worship of
God." It is a phrase that has a very wide meaning. If we

understand worship of God as respect or veneration given to a king or a great being, then one person can have one image and another quite a different one. That, for me personally, is not what I understand by worship of God. It is rather the awareness, deep inside myself, that I am not here just to satisfy my own egoism, but that I belong to quite a different life, and that there is in that life, the other life, a Source which gives a meaning to everything that exists, including my existence. It is the remembrance of that Source that turns me away from my own egoism. As I see it, worship of God is the means by which man can liberate himself from his own egoism because he is putting in front of himself a Value a Meaning, that is so much greater than himself that his own attachment and obsession with himself becomes ridiculous.

This turning of our attention towards that Source which is infinitely greater and more significant than ourselves allows the stream of life to flow through us. In doing so, it unties the knot of egoism around which all our various psychic defects are built. It certainly cannot do that quickly, because egoism is not simply a private defect that I have, that you have. All of us, in effect, really live, if not simply for our own satisfaction, at least in such a way that we feel that what is happening to us is the most important. We are not really able to enter into and feel that what happens to others is just as important as what happens to us. When man begins to feet that, then he is already beginning to be free from this general psychic defectiveness, and he begins, instead of having a sense of separation from his fellow-beings, to feel his unity with them. This comes about not because man turns towards his fellow-men, but because he is turning towards that which is supremely significant. With that turning, there comes about a certain transformation of his nature, including his body and his psyche. When it reaches a certain point, it merges with his spiritual consciousness and then he begins not only to see why he is here, but also to receive the power to perform the task for which he came. In our dealings with children, we should, therefore, constantly remember and worship God, for this will ensure that the third element in their preparation — the preservation of spiritual recollection — will be kept intact.

I do not suggest that we should concern ourselves only with the spiritual meaning. If that were true, then there would be no reason why we should be here on this earth. It is a great mistake to look upon this earthly life as if it were a mere waste of time, as if we were to say: "How soon can I throw off this mortal coil and get back to the Reality from which I came?" Life is not like that. We are here on the earth for a very important purpose. When we deal with children, we must never forget that their life on the earth is something significant; there are not here just to get through it and escape. They are here to do something. Therefore, the first part of education, the right and harmonious development of the instruments of earthly life, is the first of our responsibilities towards children. If we neglect that because we think other things are more important, we are really depriving the child of the means of living his earthly life properly. But if, on the other hand, we do not have the purpose of it all clear enough for ourselves and constantly growing clearer, then we are preparing the instruments for no purpose at all, to serve for nothing, as one might say; to build a factory that never will have anything that it can send out, but merely will keep its own machinery ticking over.

It does seem, however, that it is very difficult for people to accomplish this three-fold task in front of children unless they have help from some source which will balance these three requirements. I will repeat the three requirements: the right preparation of the natural instruments, the purification of the defects in the nature of man, and consciousness of the meaning and purpose of his own existence. Subud is one way*– I am very far from thinking or believing that it is the only way – by which those of us who have the problem really at heart can receive help in the fulfillment of our responsibilities as parents and teachers.

QUESTIONS

Q. If a child of sixteen or seventeen hears about Subud and asks, "What is Subud?" how could one reply?
Mr. Bennett: If Pak Subuh himself was asked this question, he would probably say something like, "Subud is the way to the true worship of God." This is no doubt a true and sufficient answer, but unfortunately, the words "worship" and "God" have all kinds of associations in people's minds, especially in those of young people, and they may not accept them. Therefore, we have to find some way of speaking so that we can convey this.

It is no good thinking that we can find some short, effective phrase for answering a question of this sort, because whatever phrase we use, the words will have associations and we shall probably convey the wrong thing. You have to get the feel of the particular boy or girl who is in front of you and recognize, if you can, from what in him or her the question comes. You reply to that. Probably they really want answers to some of the questions I have been discussing: "Why? What is it all for? What do we live for? How is it that we do not know this?" And perhaps a little explanation about the difference between education and preparation of the instruments and coming to know what it is, why we are doing it all, may help.

I would certainly say, especially with young people, that I would avoid any formula, however accurate it might be. When we use formulas we assume that the words we use in the formula will really convey what we

*Bennett writes of his experiences with Subud and of his decision to return to Gurdjieff's methods in his autobiography, Witness, published by Claymont Communications.

are after. Almost certainly the words that we should use in describing Subud briefly would fail to convey this.

Very often boys and girls say, "I do not want to behave as I do, but I find I cannot help myself. It is no use telling me what I *ought* to do, what I want you to tell me is how I *can* do it." If the question presents itself in that form, then, it seems to me, it is possible to come directly to Subud and say, "This is a way in which you can get help. If you know what you want to be and how you want to live, but you realize there is something in you which is unable to, then you can understand that you need some kind of inward help, and this is a way of getting that inward help." In some cases there can be as direct an approach as that.

Q. Do you think we would want children if we were free of egoism?

Mr. Bennett: Why not? We certainly should, because it is evident that part of man's task here on the earth is to ensure the continuance of the human race to do the work that is needed on the earth. If you see any kind of instrument, you know that instrument has been made for a purpose. If man has been given the power to produce children, he has been given this power for a purpose. That purpose is a duty that has nothing to do with egoism. It might even be true to say that, on the whole, in the procreation of children men and women are less egoistic than in most things. They very often forget their own convenience and comfort. Certainly it should be so. No! It is no more true to say that if we were free from egoism we should not have children, than to say that if we were free from egoism we should stop breathing. We breathe to keep this body of ours alive, and there may be a lot of egoism in that, but even a person completely free from egoism would still breathe.

Q. It has been said in the course of these lectures that we should not pretend, in front of our children, to be other

than we are. It has also been said that we should try to
rectify our defects. Cannot we, in the process of recti-
fying our defects, in effect also be hiding them?

Mr. Bennett: I take it you mean that if you are untidy
and you are busily trying to be tidy, you may give the
impression to a child that you are pretending to be tidy,
or that there is something not true about it.

Q. Yes, something like that.

Mr. Bennett: I think the first thing is never to make excuses to children, never to explain that one did so and so
"because," when the child probably knows very well
that you did it not because of that at all. Sincerity creates confidence, and not hiding defects seems to me to
be quite compatible with struggling to overcome them.
For example, I may say, "I am very untidy and I am
trying to be tidier," and the children around me will see
just how successful or unsuccessful I am in this. But
this is not really the whole story; I believe that there is
something more in all this.

The extent to which we can remedy defects by struggling with them is limited, and both we and children
should recognize this to be true. If we try to force children into a certain moral mold by acting on them, very
often we simply drive a trouble from one place to another. You drive the poison away from this place, but it
comes up again somewhere else. That is why correctional
procedures are so uncertain, why they can produce very
bad results. If that is true about children, it is true to a
great extent about ourselves. The memory of the failure
of puritanism, and the reaction against puritanism that
remains with us in our English history, is connected with
the lesson that the attempt to produce moral people by
force does not work.

This lesson has been learned over and over again, and
perhaps is now beginning to be a little better understood.
But that does not mean that we can be content to remain
in the condition that we are. As I see it, where any kind

of struggle with our own faults is concerned, the real benefit of such a struggle is more to keep us aware and conscious of our own defective nature, to enable us to see ourselves as we really are, than to produce great changes. Here I am not talking about Subud, because Subud relies entirely upon an inner working to produce the correction of the defects. If I struggle with a defect, and I do so in an honest way, I shall see a great deal more about myself than if I had not struggled; and it is the seeing that is more important, more effectual, than the actual change, the eradication of this or that bad habit. By *seeing*, man himself changes, and not merely psychic or bodily habits. Seeing is a property of the inner self, the spiritual man, and the more we see ourselves, the more we shall have the right state in front of children. If we see ourselves as we really are, we shall evoke their confidence, and that confidence is a very important factor in their accepting that something needs to change in them.

Of course, I am not talking about the kind of constant self-denigration that pities itself and says that one is "no good." This does not produce confidence either, because it is not even honest. Everything is in the middle; anything, however right, when it is pushed to an extreme leads to disaster. So I certainly do not mean anything that is exaggerated. I simply mean that if we can only remember not to make excuses, not to explain, not to be surreptitious about the wrong things that we do that our children may be aware of, then we shall gain their confidence. As far as the working within their own psychic nature is concerned, the more we wish sincerely to see ourselves and not be in a state of self-deception, the more this will keep alive in children a similar feeling; and if they are still young enough for this to be effective, then they certainly will benefit.

All this is not very difficult once one sets oneself to it. People get into the habit, unfortunately, of thinking they have to pretend in front of children and they become almost helpless not to continue pretending.

Q. I cannot see any difference between the Subud approach and the Christian approach except that the Christian has the benefit, the advantage, of a direct access to Christ, to the saving grace of Christ.

Mr. Bennett: There is only one thing that I would say about this: that a Christian must be a Christian, and it is a very difficult thing to be a Christian in truth. It is not enough to call oneself a Christian, and it is not even enough to do what the Church requires of us. There is another difficulty, you know, that the pure spiritual consciousness is only half reached so long as we have any images. Every kind of form is only a means to get to what is beyond form — because certainly God is beyond all forms. This is Christian teaching, but it is not an easy thing to remember and live that way. If a Christian remembers the words of Christ, "No man cometh to the Father except through me," he must remember that it is to come to the Father about whom nothing can be said, and about whom nothing is said in the Creed, because there is no means of saying anything. That is God beyond form.

What I have seen to be a very great benefit to people in this time and age in Subud is that it is a simple action that does not ask of people any particular form or belief beyond a willingness to turn from their own egoism towards the supreme Source. It is that deep willingness to turn away from oneself towards God that is needed, but it is not necessary that the turning away from the self — which is the meaning of the word "repentance" — should have any particular form in it. Once there is repentance, then it is said, "The kingdom of heaven is at hand," but the repentance is the key; that is, this turning, turning from self-worship to God worship. But you understand, if you start talking about such things to children, you will only confuse them.

Q. At what age can we tell children about Subud? When can we begin to answer their questions?

Mr. Bennett: Children will inevitably ask questions, and I would in no way suggest that there should be refusal to answer children's questions. But we have to learn how to answer questions without causing confusion, because what is behind the question is usually very simple. We think that they are asking about something complicated and give them a complicated answer.

For example, there may be some fears in a child that cannot be dealt with only through human assurances, and it may be quite sufficient for a child to hear you say, "You have God's protection." No more than that is needed, no explanations about it. I have seen how simply and convincingly that can work, and what looked like an elaborate question about man and God, and death and darkness and so on, is nothing else but a need for the assurance that we are under protection. That is an example that everyone can recognize, but nearly always an extremely simple answer is sufficient for children's questions, and if we keep to simple answers we shall not confuse them. Sometimes the answers, to us, may seem pretentious. How dare we answer in such a way: "Yes, you are under God's protection?" But this is true, and this is what the child needs to know, and nothing else will serve. Later, the questions begin to concern different things: For example, after thirteen or fourteen years they will really be concerned with the "why" of life. "What am I here for?" And again, this has to be answered simply, not by explanations. We may say, "There is a purpose in your life which you will have to find, and that is why you are here," or something like that. But it has to be done in such a way that what we say does not arouse a whole lot of doubts, because there are doubts in our own minds. I do not think that there is any necessity for more than this. Of course, there are the teachings of religion that do not concern me in this lec-

ture. To explain these is the duty of those who are
teachers of religion. They have to decide what should and
should not be taught to children. Nevertheless, I believe
that the central needs can be satisfied by very simple
things, mainly concerned with the way we live.

Q. Do you consider that we should teach young children
to pray?

Mr. Bennett: I think this is a matter of the mother's own
feelings, and she should be guided by that. If she does not
feel sincerely that prayer is right for the child and she
does it simply as a duty, she may only produce confusion
in the child. If she sincerely feels that prayer is good and
right for the child, even if she does not undestand it,
teaching him to pray will probably be good. What she
must not do is anything which is false to herself. That is
all. Those wo do not believe in prayer should not teach
their children to pray; those who do believe in prayer
should teach their children to pray.

Q. It seems to me that we cannot teach children anything about spiritual things. They judge entirely by the
way we live. We have not told our children about Subud,
but one day I asked our youngest what she thought
Subud had done for us. She replied, "It has made you
more loving." That was enough for me.

Mr. Bennett: Yes, that is how I see it. What is said about
this is really a matter of our response at that moment.
That is why no formula can serve. Mind you, I think it
is only fair to the audience not to give the impression
that the people who practice Subud turn rapidly into
angels, that their children are in wonderment at what
marvelous beings they have been lucky enough to acquire. I have heard children ask quite different kinds of
questions like, "How long has *he* been in Subud? Hasn't
he changed yet?

The great thing is that children are able to speak like
that, for it is a sign of confidence. I cannot picture anything that is of more value than confidence between

children and grown-up people. We can see the lengths we should go to maintain confidence. We can look back to our own childhood or watch the children of our friends and see that there is a period, between seven and eleven, when either confidence is kept or it will go. The child goes into the wilderness if that link of confidence is broken during those years. And the secret of confidence does seem to me to be simply not hiding.

Lecture 9

Spiritual Adolescence —
a Catholic Viewpoint

Father Hugh S. Thwaites

If you have been following the course of these lectures, you will indeed have found them interesting. I certainly have. And I should like to express my gratitude to my predecessors on this platform. It has been enlightening to hear these different points of view. Nevertheless, at times I found them hard to follow because the terminology was not what I am used to. And yet again, it was interesting to hear familiar concepts put in unfamiliar phrases.

Tonight, for the first time in this series of lectures, you are listening to a Catholic viewpoint. And it seems to me that I should assume that many of you are as ignorant of Catholic belief and terminology as I was of some of the matter of previous lectures. Before I come to speak of the modern child, and his hunger and aptitude for God, I think I must first put before you very briefly those aspects of Catholic belief which bear on our problem. Otherwise, you will not easily understand the point of what I say later. After that introduction, I shall deal with the causes of spiritual hunger in general. Then thirdly, I shall discuss why it is that so many children nowadays fail to come to spiritual maturity. Lastly, I shall suggest some remedies.

First, then, a sort of thumbnail sketch of some aspects of the Catholic faith:

We believe in God. To be more precise, we believe in the God of Abraham, Isaac, and Jacob. We believe in the personal God who called Abraham out of Ur of the Chaldees, who spoke to Moses on Mount Sinai, who chose David to be king.

We believe that this God exists from all eternity, before there was ever space or time. He created angels, pure spirits, and called them to live in his presence, to love and praise Him forever. He allowed them some sort of testing before He would admit them to His presence. In this testing, some of the Angels turned away from Him in rebellion. He condemned the rebellious angels to everlasting punishment.

God also created space and all it contains, including this world. And God created man. Although we may allow that the body of the first man on this planet evolved from simpler beings, his soul, like the soul of every man who has ever lived, was directly created by God.

We are, then, partly body and partly spirit. Matter and spirit are utterly unlike, even opposed, in their nature. Nevertheless, when God first made man, he joined matter and spirit together, and so marvelously that all the faculties of the mind and body worked together in harmony. The body and the lower faculties of the soul were completely obedient to reason and the will.

Man's reason and will were in turn obedient to God's law. All was harmony, as it might be in a ship's crew where each does his task for the common good, all being guided by the will and mind of the captain, who in turn is obeying his superior at home.

As with the angels, God wanted man, too, to live in his presence and love and praise him forever. And as with the angels, He allowed our common ancester some sort of testing. In this testing, man failed. He disobeyed God.

That failure, that fall, that original sin, profoundly affects the modern child. It profoundly affects you and me.

For it was as though the captain had disobeyed his superior at home, and the crew, catching the spirit of rebellion, had broken out in mutiny. If the captain, by his own irresponsible behavior, loses control of his crew, each member of it following his own whim, there is disharmony on board, and all suffer in consequence.

So too, when the first man on this planet, by his sin of disobedience, turned his will, the *key* faculty, away from God, the harmony in human nature was lost. Each sense began to seek its own satisfaction regardless of the others, regardless of the good of the whole man. It is because the passions are so heedless of the light of reason that they are called "blind." And so began the conflict between "the flesh" and "the spirit."

I hope you are with me so far. It is because of the original sin of the first man that we are gathered here tonight. But for that original sin, the modern child would not know spiritual hunger. His appetite for God would be perpetually and completely satisfied. But that sin of the first man has left his descendants with dimmed intellect and weakened will, and their senses a mutinous crew.

However, Christians believe that God did not leave men in this plight. We believe that among the descendants of Abraham and David was a girl called Mary, who conceived when still a virgin. Her child, whom we call Jesus, had no human father. We believe that the ovum in her womb was miraculously fecundated by the direct action of God.

This Jesus grew up and worked many miracles to authenticate his claim to speak for God. By a word, that is to say, he would heal lepers, calm a storm at sea, or raise the dead to life. His teaching drew on him the hatred of the Jewish leaders, and they had him put to death. During his lifetime, he had frequently foretold that this would happen, but he always concluded the prophecy with the strange assertion that on the third day he would come alive again. We believe that this indeed happened, and that for forty days after his resurrection he was seen alive by many of his friends and relatives. He ate and drank and spoke with them.

Jesus claimed to be God. He taught his followers that in the Godhead there were three Persons, whom he called the Father, the Son, and the Holy Spirit. Not three gods, but one God subsisting in three Persons. This God Christians call the Blessed Trinity. Jesus claimed to be God the Son. And so we hold that the Second Person of the Blessed Trinity, who had been born of the Father before time began, was born of the Virgin Mary less than 2,000 years ago.

We hold, too, that Jesus came to do three things: to teach us about God, to satisfy divine justice for all human sin by his own sacrificial death, and to bring a new principle of life to the world. And this is where we catch up again with the modern child. For Jesus came to satisfy the spiritual hunger of all men by giving a new life to their souls. This new life makes us sharers of the divine nature, gives us a sharing in the life of Jesus Christ. It is vastly above our mere human nature, and we call it supernatural, above nature. Just as human life would be supernatural to a dog, above a dog's nature, so this new life I am speaking of is supernatural to us, above our nature.

You have heard the story, perhaps, of the cinema manager who looked into the theater during a showing, just to make sure they weren't ripping up the seats or setting fire to the place. As he looked around, he saw a dog sitting there. He was just going to go up to its owner to tell him to take it out when, to his astonishment, he saw the dog laugh. So he went on observing, and saw that the dog was obviously following the film with great interest. When the show was over, he followed the man out and said to him, "Your dog seemed to be enjoying that film." "Yes," said the man, "it's funny; he didn't like the book at all."

Some people idolize their dogs. They give them the best chairs in the house, and so on. When they start kissing them and addressing half their conversation to them, we say that really they are going too far. A dog, we say, is after all only a dog, however attractive it may be.

Yet God has gone even further than this in his love for men. There is obviously a far greater disproportion between God and man than any two of his creatures could have between themselves. Yet God, we say, has given us, through Jesus, a share in his own divine nature.

As a seed, placed in a pot of earth, strikes root and grows into a plant by assimilating into itself elements out of the soil, so, we say, did Jesus come into this world, a solitary seed of divine life. And he died in order that he might be a new principle of life to all men. Just as the seed planted in the soil must die as a seed before it can live as a plant, so did Jesus die as a man in order that others might come to life in him.

We say, then, that a man lives this new life in Jesus, much as a molecule taken up out of the soil lives in the plant. So that a man is living, you may say, two lives: his merely human life by which his soul is joined to his body, and his divine life by which he is joined to God.

Another way of looking at the same thing is to say that God comes into the soul of a man and thereby causes it to live with this new life. Just as the air in this hall is bright because of the presence of so many lights, so we say that it is the indwelling of God in the human soul which makes it start living with this supernatural life.

Although I have been talking from the Christian point of view, this supernatural life is, of course, offered to all men and is, indeed, possessed by all God's true friends, whatever their religion. There is only one God. If a man loves him and truly tries to please him, then God comes and dwells in him, thereby giving him this new supernatural life.

What I have said so far, then, is a thumbnail sketch of those points of Catholic belief which touch on our problem tonight. I now come to the second point.

You will have noticed that I have assumed from the start that it is God and only God who can adequately satisfy our spiritual hunger. And I am afraid that you may be thinking I am taking an unconscionable time in coming to the problem of the modern child. But since the modern child has just the same human nature that we have, it seems to me better to treat first what can satisfy the spiritual hunger of man as such, before coming to the special case of the modern adolescent.

Fulton Sheen points to God alone as being able to satisfy our spiritual hunger in the following way. Our happiness, he says, consists in fulfilling the purpose of our being. Now every man knows, from his unfulfilled hunger for them, that he was built with a capacity for three things of which he never has enough. He wants life, and not just for the next few minutes or years, but for always, and with no aging or disease to threaten it. He wants to grasp truth, and not just this truth or that truth, this subject or that subject; he wants all truth. And he wants love, with no time limit or disappointment or disillusion, but perfect and unending. In this world, however, life is shadowed by death, truth mingles with error, love is mixed with hatred. Where will he find the perfection his heart craves for? If you are looking in this world for the source of light, you do not look under a tree, where light is mixed with shadow. You look to the sun where light is pure. And if we are looking for the unadulterated source of love, life, and truth, we must go out beyond the limits of this shadowed world. Eternal life, pure truth, inebriating and unending love—this is the very definition of God.

Man, in other words, finds in God the fulfillment of all his longing.

We can come to the same conclusion in another way. God gave Moses the Ten Commandments on Mount Sinai. These commandments are like the handbook that the car manufacturer gives the purchaser, telling him what he must do and what he must not do if he wants to get the best out of his car. The Ten Commandments describe the moral laws of our nature, and tell us what to do and what not to do if we want to be happy. Just as the car manufacturer might put in his handbook, "Thou shalt not try to run this car without oil in the gearbox," so God says to us, "Thou shalt not steal." The car manufacturer is not trying to limit the freedom or enjoyment of the purchaser. He just wants him to get the most out of his car. And when God tells me that I must not bear false witness, he is not being repressive. He just wants me to be happy.

A moral law expresses what is already a law of nature. Of all the commandments, of all these moral laws to which our nature is subject, God has told us that the most important is this: that we should love God with all our heart and all our soul and all our mind and all our strength. This, apparently, is the very first thing we must do if we want to be happy.

You can make a cake without currants, but you cannot make it without flour.

It is evidently of the nature of the human heart that it should seek God. If it is not doing this, it is impossible for it to be fully, lastingly happy. After all, every creature must obey the laws of its own nature. A stone is made to fall downwards. If you throw a stone up in the air, so long as it is going up there is a sort of tension within it. When it stops going up and starts falling down again, if it could think it would realize, "This is what I'm meant to be doing." Now the human heart is meant to go towards God. Only when a person is consciously directing his life towards God does he know beyond the possibility of doubt that, "This is what I'm meant to be doing." But if a man directs his life towards some object other than God, then he is creating within himself an inner unhappiness that no psychiatrist can heal. In other words, the human soul is a capacity for God. Left unfulfilled, it experiences hunger.

I have still one or two things to say about the mechanics of this soul life before I come to the modern child.

God is good. God is holy. It is love that joins a man to God. It is sin that separates a man from God. All sin ultimately boils down to rebellion against God. To break the moral law which we find built into our conscience necessarily involves estrangement from the law giver.

Yet although God is infinitely holy and just, and serious sin at once drives him out of our hearts, he is also infinitely merciful, and our sincere repentance brings immediate reconciliation with him. If a sinner turns to God with sorrow in his heart and asks for pardon, then God forgives him. Therefore, it is highly important for the health of our souls that we should turn to God in prayer and ask his forgiveness.

To conclude this section, I should now like to summarize what I have said so far by giving five short rules of spiritual hygiene, five short rules for satisfying the spiritual hunger of Mr. Everyman.

1. If he wants to be happy, he must let God come into his life. He must be a friend of God. If he is on good terms with God, he will have peace of soul. If God has no place in his life, he may search for peace of soul, but he will never find it. His spiritual hunger will endure.

2. This is how to find God and be his friend. God is a spirit. (A Christian will object, "But God became Man." Yes, but what I am saying now can be of use to anyone, whatever his religion.)

3. If a man wants to find God and have peace of soul, he must pray. He should spend at least a minute on his

knees every night. Kneeling down expresses the attitude of adoration a man should have when speaking to God.

4. Since love joins us to God and sin separates us from him, a man might pray like this: "I love you, my God, above all things, and I repent with all my heart of having offended you. Never permit me to separate myself from you again. Grant that I may love you always, and then do with me what you will."

5. Lastly, just as food, drink, exercise, and sleep are necessary for the health of your body, prayer is necessary for the health of your soul. So a man must make himself be faithful to prayer. He should pray seriously at least once a day, before he goes to bed. He should talk to God in his own words. He is our Father, and does not look for fine speeches. He looks for sincerity, for humility, for the longing of your heart for him. St. Augustine said, "Thou hast made us for thyself, O God, and our hearts are restless till they rest in thee."

I now come to the third part of my talk: spiritual adolescence.

What are the special difficulties that face our children today? Why is it, at least as far as Catholic children are concerned, so many in our cities fall away from all religious practice, fall away from the life of the spirit, so soon after leaving school?

I will deal with this problem from various aspects. First I shall consider what effect technical progress may have had on the spiritual life of children.

There has been much discussion in recent times on the influence that technical advances have had on the mentality of men today, and on the dangers that thereby threaten their moral and spiritual values. Needless to say, children are exposed in very much the same way. Technical progress can greatly change their spiritual and interior life, their relationship with God and all that concerns the supernatural, especially since they accept these impressions much more easily than do grown-ups, without any reflection or opposition, and they are formed by these influences.

I will explain what I mean. Children's development depends a great deal on their surroundings and on their contact with nature (plants, animals, mountains, rivers, the sea, the stars, and so on) or on their contact with the mechanical side of life. The latter is man-made, while the former is discovered by children without their seeing who made it.

The things of nature, such as plants and animals, grow and move about, and there is a sense of mystery about them, something which cannot clearly be grasped by us. This sense of mystery is lacking in the case of machines. We can get to know them to the last component, we can find out who made them, how they were made, how they work. Seeing the things of nature, children are easily led to the knowledge of the Creator, of the good God who is our Father.

Seeing machines does not lead them, at least directly, to think of God the Creator. Machines can be broken down into parts and then put back together again. You can study all their mechanism, how they work. The things of nature, on the other hand, once destroyed cannot be put together again. And so the more dealings children have with machines, the less will they appreciate the mystery of life. They do not learn that reverence towards creation which is so important if they are to have a true reverence towards the Creator.

Children today perhaps are losing this sense of admiration, this sense of wonder at creation. And so we often come across the type of child who is blase, with a sort of childish sophistication. Such a child no longer learns with wonder to admire the greatness and the beauty of nature, and especially he is no longer led from creatures to the Creator.

To this danger is added another. Children are brought up today in the society of men formed by a technical age, men who live according to the principles of utilitarianism. Machines are measured only by their utility. Things have value only in so far as they help to make a man's life more comfortable, more gracious. This utilitarianism is the greatest enemy of the idealism to which children are naturally so well disposed. Either it suffocates all idealism, or it subordinates it to comfort, progress, and materialistic values, or else it leads to an idealism directed to false ends and so withdraws it from the service of God. In all of these, the soul of the child suffers real, and often irreparable harm, because this basic power of the soul, the power to love, is withdrawn from giving itself fully to the good and the true, and from serving God with all its strength.

These two dangers and their consequences, which we can see among children, are often not guarded against. Indeed, on the contrary, parents and teachers are accustomed to praise this practical, utilitarian, hard-boiled, worldly sense in children. It promises that they will get on well in life, and grown-ups deplore its absence.

Yet I would say that this mentality, although it is completely blameless in children, constitutes a great obstacle to their spiritual formation. This utilitarian, sophisticated attitude makes profound religious experience very difficult, and so, ordinarily, their spiritual life remains undeveloped. In matters of human love, if a person maintains this self-centered attitude, he will never come to real love. So, too, with real religion. After all, what is this life but a drawn-out love affair that we have with God, in which God keeps giving us ever fresh proof of his love, and we are invited to an ever deeper intimacy with him?

Another special difficulty our children face is their social life. More than the rest of us, young people are like sheep, they follow the gang. They are led by example, and are much more sensitive to human respect than they will be later in life.

One might say that it is a function of those who govern to foster convention and observance so that the general drift of the crowd is towards God. That is to say, the general atmosphere should be such as would favor normal spiritual development. Such, however, is far from being the case in British cities. There, the atmosphere is thoroughly pagan, thoroughly materialistic. If a young person wants to remain loyal to his spiritual convictions, he must be ready to go it alone. Where social pressure should aid our school-leavers, it fails them. Where it should foster and encourage their spiritual evolution, it bitterly opposes it.

From this social aspect, what makes normal spiritual adolescence harder today than it used to be is the licentious nature of so much of our press and television. Earlier lecturers have dwelt on this point, so I will not pursue the matter. But with inborn concupiscence aided by so much propaganda, what wonder that so many of our young people break the moral law and so break their spiritual life? For clearly there is an intimate connection between the observance of the moral law and spiritual health. Spiritual health comes from having right relations with God. To break the moral law is to offend the Law-giver. Moral disorder and spiritual disorder are linked together, as cause and effect.

When young people fall away from religious observance, it is, in my experience, most often because there has been a moral fall-away. It is sin rather than syllogisms that turns people atheists. When fish rot, the process starts in their head. When men go rotten, the process starts in their heart.

So much for the social or moral aspect of the problem. From the psychological point of view, we can say that young people who fall away from any living of the spiritual life do so because they have never personally grasped its meaning. They have been living it, but have not understood it.

This, for Christians, can be expressed in theological terms by saying that while they have had the **gift** of faith, they have never had the **light** of faith. A Christian, as soon as he is baptised, possesses the gift of faith. But this should develop with his developing intellect until he has a personal appreciation of the truth of what his religion teaches him.

A comparison might help to show what I mean. There are water heaters that always have a tiny flame burning— a pilot light. When you turn the water on, the gas is turned on, too, and this tiny flame becomes a great roaring flame that fills the whole cylinder. You could blow out the tiny flame, but you could never blow the flame out when the heater has been turned on.

The gift of faith is like that little pilot flame. While the person is a child, this flame is safe. But if, by the time the child leaves school, this tiny flame has not developed into a strong fire of the knowledge and love of God, then the first blast of ridicule or skepticism will be enough to blow it out.

For Christians there is a further point on this same subject. One way of explaining the big fall-away of our school children from the beliefs in which they were brought up is by saying that they have never really come to know Jesus Christ as a person. They have learned **about** him, of course. But there is a vast difference between knowing about a person and knowing him. I know quite a lot about the Queen. But I do not know her.

Christianity started off by being simply the knowing and loving and following of Jesus Christ. And this personal love of Jesus has always been the secret strength of the mature Christian. If our young people grow up without growing in intimacy with Christ, what wonder that their religion would come to seem cold and empty? It is the attractiveness of Jesus and the charm of his friendship that largely makes the Christian religion enjoyable.

A third way of putting the same thing is to say that

those young people who fall away from the practice of their religion have never surmounted the crisis of spiritual puberty. Not everyone goes through this crisis, but many do. In May last year, I was talking to a boy of eighteen in a Scottish grammar school. He had been intending to go on for the priesthood, but now felt that he couldn't. It seemed to him, he said, that he could no longer accept the truths of the Catholic faith until he had verified them for himself, one by one. It had seemed his duty, he said, to jettison all the articles of his religion, and examine them piecemeal to test whether he could accept them or not.

I explained to him that what was happening to him was a normal stage in many people's spiritual development. There was no quick way of getting out of it. You just had to live through it, like measles. I told him that he was going the right way about surmounting the crisis, namely more intensive study. But I told him that he should also increase the time given to prayer. Study alone would never get him out of his present difficulty. But if he studied quite sincerely and prayed humbly, he would probably be quite all right in six months time, and would have greatly profited by the experience. As it turned out, it was only three months later that he wrote to me and said that everything was now all right, and that he was going to the seminary.

I call this a sort of spiritual puberty, because it mostly happens during a person's teens. When his intellect is coming to full strength, a boy is conscious of its power. Naturally and rightly he applies it to all that he sees and knows. And of course he applies it to the truths of his religion. But faith is a gift. (I am speaking now about the Christian religion.) Faith is a gift, a freely-given sharing in the knowledge of God, and the unaided human intellect cannot grasp the mysteries it holds. And so there is a sense of floundering.

If a boy going through this crisis gives up on prayer,

then indeed he will come to reject his religion. Divine truths must be approached prayerfully, humbly. If a man approaches the study of God in the same attitude as he might approach, say, the study of beetles, then the more he studies God the further he will be from God. "God resists the proud, but gives grace to the humble."

I now come to the last point that bears on the question of why so many young people fall away from their religion. The spiritual life, like all forms of life, needs nourishment. The soul feeds off God. Just as the proper object of the stomach is food, of the ear sound and harmony, of the eye light and color, of the mind truth; so the soul needs God. We establish contact with God and draw nourishment from him in prayer. Therefore, if children do not pray, inevitably their spiritual life will languish. Not praying will not, of itself, kill the spiritual life. Only serious sin does this. But the absence of any prayer-life will so weaken the spiritual life that it will be unable to meet the onslaughts of a pagan world.

In the case of our bodies, people don't die of starvation. If they are starved, they die of some sickness which, because of their starved condition, they are unable to resist. During the war, when I was a prisoner of war in Siam, many of our people died. They died of beriberi, malaria, dysentery, cholera. But the root cause was always starvation. In one camp I was in, two-thirds of our number died in one month. If we had had enough to eat, they would not have died. But starvation had lowered their bodily resistance so that they could not withstand the infection. They succumbed through want of physical vitality.

If people do not pray, their spiritual life is thereby weakened. They meet with some temptation, they breathe the atmosphere of a pagan world, and through sheer want of spiritual vitality they succumb. Through want of prayer they have allowed their own interior re-

sistance to be lowered to a dangerous degree. And so
their spiritual life is extinguished. Another victory for
a materialistic world. And so if our boys and girls grow
up without prayer, inevitably their spiritual life will be
at a low ebb. What food and drink is to the body, prayer
is to the soul. And so if they don't pray, how can they
hope to survive?

For Catholics, there is one more way of drawing
strength and life from God, namely the sacraments.
When I am going around Catholic schools, I tell the
children that they need to go to Holy Communion at
least once a week. Any Catholic school teacher will
tell you of the great effect frequent Holy Communion
has on children. And also, for Catholic children, frequent confession does a great deal to help them safely
through the reefs of adolescence.

To sum up this last point, then, I would say that one
main cause for shipwreck during spiritual adolescence
is simply spiritual malnutrition. The spiritual life is
more or less starved to death.

I now come to the last part of what I have to say: What
should we be doing to prevent the modern child dying
of spiritual hunger? Already I have pointed the way to
this. So I will now suggest just three points.

First, we should keep doing what lies in our power to
make society less pagan, less materialistic, less hostile to
spiritual ideals. For instance, there is the tolerance of
pornography and those who make money from it. In
Britain, we largely seem to let smut-peddlers get away
with it. At least, you could not say that there is a nation-
wide campaign against them. Existing legislation could be
enforced more rigidly, and tighter laws could be passed.
And this is just one example of an abuse that flourishes
with relatively little hindrance.

There are many others. The normal talk in many a
factory and office is degrading. An apprentice once told
me that the conversation around him at work was sometimes so hellish that he simply had to go into the lavatory

in order to pray. That's pathetic. I know it's easy for me to talk, fortified as I am by a Roman collar. But all the same, the world is becoming more and more obviously divided into two camps: materialists, and those who believe in spiritual realities. And each person should make it quite plain to all concerned which side he is on.

The second remedy I would put forward is that parents should take more to heart their duty of giving their children adequate sex instruction. It is the parents' duty. To let their children find these things out for themselves is to ask for danger. To allow children to reach puberty without having warned them of what is going to happen to them, without warning them of the intrinsic dangers, without warning them of dangers that may come from without, is wrong and culpable. If a father or mother refrains from telling their children the things they need to know, on the grounds, "Oh, well, they'll soon find out," the children will find out, and it will be too late.

As I've said, moral disorder causes spiritual disorder. And so if young people are not pure, they will scarcely learn how to satisfy their spiritual hunger. If they do not cope adequately with physical adolescence, they will not cope adequately with spiritual adolescence. God knows what is in man, and he knew what he was saying when he told us, "Blessed are the pure in heart, for they shall see God."

Thirdly, parents and all who deal with children should teach them to pray, show them how to pray. Let them see you praying, and let them join you in talking to God. Let them see from an early age what importance you attach to prayer. In those early years, before the intellect develops, the subconscious is, so to speak, wide open, and is storing impressions that will never be lost. They will not be remembered in after years, but nevertheless—indeed, on that very account—they will be deeply formative.

I will end on this note, that prayer is the key to the

satisfying of all man's spiritual hunger. God, who made us, has left us with this void in our hearts which only he can fill. The appetites, the desires of the human heart are infinite. Only God can satisfy them. And God satisfies them effortlessly. We open our hearts to God in prayer.

Therefore, show children how to pray, help them to pray, give them a liking for prayer. If you do this, they will soon taste and see that the Lord is sweet. When a baby is hungry, it is discontented, fractious, crying. When it is at the breast, it is happy, it is quiet and contented. Show a child how he may find God, and you will have shown him how to satisfy his spiritual hunger—not only in this life, but forever.

QUESTIONS

Q. I see three causes of falling away: (1) If one has no actual experience of grace. How can someone who is not in touch with God bring a child to God? (2) The falling off is chiefly among the Christians rather than among the Jews and Moslems. I am a Jew, but even if I wanted to accept Christianity, I should find it difficult to believe in the virgin birth, and in Christ as the only Son of God. It is difficult to accept; it is in the nature of a legend. (3) The most serious cause is, I believe, that there is no lead in the churches on the really important moral questions. The Quakers stand up firmly for their principles, for pacifism, but not the other Christian sects.

Father Thwaites: With regard to the first point, about bringing children in touch with God, it seems not to be all that hard. I have come across many cases of young children with a real love for God. God exists, and he lives in us, and he is all love, and he wants nothing so much as that we should love him, and if people start turning towards God, then God is not backward. God does not leave it to be a one-sided love affair. In fact, it is mostly the other way around, God making all the effort and man doing just about nothing. So if a child really does start trying to please God and love God and get to know God, then God certainly rewards that child by making his presence felt unmistakably. And that happens time and again with children I have known. God is somebody very real, for whom they have a real love. I have a small niece. When she kisses people she likes especially, she gives them a hug. When she was five years old, she said, "When I get to heaven, I am going to hug God, I love him so." To her God was somebody as real as her mother, and she used to pray to God often during the day, and when things went wrong, there she started praying. That happens with many, many children. If they are taught to pray from the time they are two years old, then God does discover himself to them, and there is no doubt about the reality of what has happened to them. They know that God loves them.

Your second point was about the trimmings in our faith, the bits and pieces apart from the mere existence of God. In point of fact, people do not seem to find these a difficulty, and in my experience, it is not these trimmings which make people fall away. The reason I have given for the fall away is sheer malnutrition through want of prayer. This, in my experience, is the main reason, not matters of dogma, not intellectual difficulties.

Thirdly, you spoke about the Church giving a lead on moral questions. The Church exists to fit people into eternal life. It does other things, too, perhaps, but its job is to try to guide people with God in this life so that when this world packs up or when they die, then they are found ready to live in the eternal life for which they are made. So the Church admittedly has its eyes on eternity, and only secondarily on this world. The main thing that the Church tries to deal with is sin.

Q. But what about war? Is it not always wrong to kill?

Father Thwaites: In point of fact, there is such a thing

as a just war, but perhaps this is just a red herring. It is better to leave pacifists to go their own good way in peace and people who think they do right in fighting a just war, let them fight it. And perhaps both sides will save their eternal souls. In heaven we will all be pacifists.

Q. Can you say more about the teaching on original sin in the Church? In the maternity hospital, the girl in the bed next to me was a Roman Catholic. When her child was brought to her for the first time to feed, she was very upset, and said, "This child is very wicked," and refused to feed it. Perhaps in the teaching there is too much emphasis on original sin?

Father Thwaites: That sounds absolutely fantastic. I never have heard of such a thing before. I would not have believed it possible, but there you are. She must have been a bit odd, or maybe she did not feel well after having had her baby. It is obviously wrong, it is not the teaching of the Church.

Q. But does it not follow from original sin? She may have been told that newborn children are depraved.

Father Thwaites: Yes, obviously. She must have got hold of the wrong end of quite a few sticks. We believe that when children are born, they are deprived of that eternal life which God wants to give them. St. Paul calls them "children of wrath, enemies of God," and to some extent they are under the domination of Satan. Baptism changes all that and makes them Sons of God. She was right in saying that her child was to some extent bad; not through its own fault, obviously, but through the fault of the First Man. That whole business of original sin is about the most mysterious dogma of our faith, altough it is one of the most important. But when children are born, certainly, to some extent, they are enemies of God because they are born into a race which has rebelled against God.

Q. I wonder if I could ask Father Thwaites to take up the question of prayer, because it has arisen two or three times in the course of these lectures. When I was speaking last week, this question was put to me, about teaching children to pray, and earlier the question was put, "If parents are themselves without faith, and acknowledge themselves to be without faith, can they really teach their children to pray? Will it really be prayer that is taught?" You have spoken throughout the evening about prayer as if it was always effective, but is there not a certain inner quality, a certain intention that must be present in prayer for it to be effective and not to be the mere prayer of the mind and prayer of the lips? It is this effective prayer, it seems to me, about which you are speaking. But how is effective prayer to be conveyed to children by parents—as so many are—who feel their own spiritual hunger, but have not themselves any confidence in the reality of prayer? They feel doubtful about whether they are entitled to teach children to pray. I put myself in your hands now, because I was asked this question last week, and I replied, "If a mother believes in prayer, she should teach her child to pray, but if she does not believe in prayer, she should not teach her child to pray because she would be teaching the child a lie." If I was wrong in that, I hope you will correct me.

Father Thwaites: If you do not believe in prayer yourself, you would not be able to teach a child to pray. No one can give what he does not have. I think a distinction might help here. We have these two faculties: intellect and will. These two faculties of the soul are like two arms which reach out to embrace reality. When man is studying, it is his intellect which is the more important faculty. His will is important because it must apply him to his study even when he does not want to study, but it is with his intellect that he penetrates the subject and makes it his own. When a man prays, on the other hand, it is his will which is the more important faculty. His intellect tells him why he should love God, why he should hate sin, but with his will he says to God, "I love you," and that is the important thing.

In a way, it is like a needle and a thread. The needle

goes in beforehand to prepare the way for the thread, but it is the thread that binds the two pieces of cloth together. With my intellect, I see why I should love God, but with my will I say to him, "I love you." It is that which unites me to God. And if a man just reasons about divine things but does not use his will, then he is like a person sewing without a thread in the needle: It is just a waste of time. And so, when we are praying, it is not just a matter of speaking about things, but using the heart: adoration, love, gratitude, detestation of sin, asking pardon for sin—these are the important things.

Suppose two people were going to have meditation about sin, prayer about sin, and one man had enough marvelous ideas about sin to write a whole treatise on sin, and the other just thought, "My God, have mercy on me, a sinner." Obviously, the second man is making a good prayer and the first man is not making a good prayer. And so in the middle of prayer, it is important to bear in mind the distinction between the intellect and the will, these two separate faculties, and to use the will rather than the intellect. In prayer, we can use the intellect only to feed matter on which the will can work.

But as for a mother who does not believe in prayer, I think she would be quite incapable of teaching her children to pray, and I think she should find somebody who does believe in prayer. Or, better still, learn how to pray herself and learn to believe in it. Because once a person has tried to pray, they will believe in it, because God, after all, is looking for the least excuse to help people. And if people turn to God in humility and sincerity, then God will not be backward. And so I say, if parents do not personally believe in payer, then they should try praying, and they will come to believe in prayer.

The great difference in the human race, no matter what religion men are, lies ultimately in whether a man prays or whether he does not pray. That is the important thing in life, and for these children. I say again that this is what they chiefly need, and this is where they are mainly lacking: They lead lives without prayer.

Q. I think this is a theme that has been running through all the lectures. You have spoken about the supernatural element in prayer. It is not just what we do as human beings—as you have just said this moment—prayer is also what God does for us. Then you spoke about this little girl who said that when she goes to heaven, she will hug God as she hugs her mother. In other words, she has really formed an entirely natural anthropomorphic picture of God. She is being led towards a form of prayer which is only natural and not a supernatural prayer. Later, when the question of the supernatural element arises, this sort of preparation which takes religion entirely on a natural level and teaches prayer with an anthropomorphic image—an image not merely of God made manifest in Christ, but of God the Father in heaven—will this not lead her into confusion? Is it not true that very often at the moment when young people awaken to the need for deeper understanding, they ask, "What is the reality?" Then they cannot remain on the anthropomorphic, natural basis that they had before, and nothing has been prepared to bring them to the wonder and mystery of prayer. Then we have the sad situation that so few people have the real sense of the mystery of our relationship with God, or the supernatural element as something that is really our own, of our own experience. How can all those people who have not got it themselves bring to children this sense of the supernatural, of the indefinable, of the mystery? I think that something like that has been running through all the questions that we have asked.

Father Thwaites: God does accomodate himself to our weakness. We know that God is completely transcendent, and infinitely above anything we can begin to imagine. Yet he does stoop to our lowness and he comes to live in a man. We can only use our own human minds to think. To have a certain imagining of God is not all that harmful because the love that we have for him now is the same sort of love we will have when we die. There, in heaven, please God it will be purified and greater, but all the same, we can now really love God. If you cannot see a person, you can still talk to them, and even though we cannot see God, we can be well aware of his presence.

A boy of nineteen was telling me how he used to say his prayers after he had gone to bed, and how he talked to God, and he said that it was especially when he was in bed at night that God seemed so close he could almost touch him. That is a reality, God is close. He is in us. To try to imagine it may help some people.

God does not expect us to pray like angels. He expects us to pray like men and women, and he is content with this, just like a father. If a man's child just gets out the first word, "Dada," the father will be very pleased and will tell everybody that his child can talk. This child can only say one word, and it is not intelligible to anyone except his father. But the father loves the child so much that he is delighted with that one poor word. And God loves us so much that even our poor, inadequate, halting, distracted prayer is a delight to God.

For my part, I always feel a great humbug when I talk about prayer because I always wish I knew how to pray properly. But I do know this, that God—in spite of our inadequate prayers—does love us, and God does not ask for success in our prayers. That is his gift: All God asks is that we should try. There is a vast difference in people's gifts of prayer, and there are many, many different ways of praying. Suppose a person gets no further all his life than saying, "My God, I love you," with his lips, out loud: "My God, I love you, help me to love you more." Already, that person is pleasing God and is going the right way. If a person stays on a low level of prayer, he should not be distressed, because prayer, after all, is not an end in itself, it is only a means to an end. And what is the end? The end is the greater glory of

God, and we contribute to that end by loving God and being as holy as he wants us to be.

Prayer is an instrument to enable us to live this eternal life, so that when we die in this world, then we shall live forever. Prayer is not an end in itself, and I have sometimes thought that if I ever learned to pray well, I would get so proud and conceited I would be insufferable. I am perfectly content to be on a very low level of prayer all my life, to be trying to learn how to pray. That is good enough, at least for saving a person's soul. To pray well is secondary: The important thing is to pray. Anybody can pray, because everyone has got a heart and can realize that God loves him. Even if people cannot go into ecstacy and be wholly eaten up with the love of God, at least they can tell God, "I am trying to love you, help me to love you more." That is an excellent prayer.

Q. How can a baby pray? Doesn't infant baptism imply prayer?

Father Thwaites: We believe that when babies are baptized, God gives them a new seed of life by virtue of the Church. And so already, the baby is living a life, even though he cannot think he is living a life. With his dawning consciousness, the child should become aware of this. If he does not, then the life is very, very feeble, like a seedling. It will die if it is not fortified through prayer. But we believe that the sacrament of baptism is enough to give children that life.

Lecture 10

A Summing-up and Practical Conclusions

J.G. Bennett

When I was faced with the task that I have tonight, I realized that I am particularly badly equipped to do it. It is one thing to ramble on about one's own ideas, but to try to grasp and put together the ideas of a number of people, coming from quite different sources, is a very different thing.

Certainly there is one thing that is very noticeable: Apparently quite inconsistent, even contradictory things were said about the very same problem. Even the two speakers who spoke from the Roman Catholic stand-point – Mario Montessori and Father Thwaites – said almost opposite things about the child. Mario Montessori said that one cannot speak of spiritual hunger in a child because a child is spirituality, and that a child does not know about spiritual problems any more than wine knows about wine. On the other hand, Father Thwaites referred to the doctrine of innate depravity. A question about original sin was put to him, and he agreed that the child is, in some way, born as the opponent of God and has to be reconciled to God through baptism. These seemed to be two points of view as different as one could possibly have on the same subject. Or again, Mr. Maung Maung Ji spoke of the child as being able to develop solely according to what is in him, according to what he has brought on to this earth, and that anything that we attempt to do or give the child will only disturb this development of an entirely natural process. On the other hand, we were told — in the lectures by both Mr. Williams and Mr. Pollack, who spoke about the connection with the Old Testament and the prophets and psalmists — that we have to make around the child a very definite environment within which his spiritual life will take a definite shape. The Steiner thesis as developed by Adam Bittleston is nearer to this than to the others.

There are many other ways in which one could set one lecture against another and say, "These people contradicted one another and nothing clear comes of it." One example I must mention refers to spiritual teaching, or religious instruction. Some people said, and I certainly said it when I had to speak on the two specialized themes of Gurdjieff and Subud, that if we try to teach children something about religion, we do something artificial which is only grafted on to the outside. The early years are not the time to learn such things, but are for learning about this world into which the child has come. That also seems to contradict what, let us say, Father Thwaites said about the importance of prayer and teaching from the very start. Adam Bittleston spoke of the importance of bringing home to the child the spiritual significance of nature, and showing in diverse ways that nature is a manifestation of divine love, divine wisdom. This means, in effect, teaching the child about spiritual things through his contact with nature.

I think that these apparent contradictions really illustrate the difficulty of dealing with things through words. As I read these lectures over and over again, I was convinced that everyone was speaking about the same thing, and even meant the same thing. The essential point on which all agreed is that spirituality cannot be taught as if it were an educational subject. I believe also that all were agreed that the child has a mixed nature: partly spiritual, partly material.

All authorities agree that there are well marked periods or ages of childhood, each of which creates its own problems: somatic, psychic, and spiritual. The first period is from conception to birth, the second from birth to six, seven, or eight years. Here our speakers have differed slightly in assigning the age of transition, but all agree that the changes are so profound that the handling of children must be entirely different before and after the change. The third phase leads to the completion of puberty. After puberty, the transition to adult life is less well-defined. It seems, from various points raised in the discussions, that the average man or woman cannot rightly be said to have "grown-up" until some age between twenty-one and twenty-four years. Our concern in these lectures has been mainly with the two periods from birth to puberty.

This does not mean that the prenatal period is not vitally important, so I shall take first the question of what we already are when we come into the world. What is a newborn child? Is he a purely spiritual being as at one point Mario Montessori seemed to suggest? He referred to the unblemished spirituality which was able to convert his mother and which does not require anything because it already has it all. From this point of view, we have robbed the child of his birthright. Or, is it right to speak, as Gurdjieff does, for example, of the child as having only the potentiality of a soul? This suggests that the child's spiritual potential may or may not be realized in this life, and its fulfillment depends entirely upon whether the external conditions are favorable or not. Or is it right to speak also in terms of natural depravity, or original sin?

I do not think that these apparently contradictory assertions are nearly so difficult to understand as they seem because they are simply putting emphasis on different aspects of the same whole. This can be seen if we turn back to the notion which is inherent in any understanding of a being such as man — that we have a three-fold nature: a spiritual nature, a soul nature, and a body nature. Our spiritual nature is strongly in evidence in earliest childhood, as described by Mario Montessori. It is a reality that can be recognized by a scientist like his mother, who sought to understand how it was that the normal child was able to respond in such an extraordinary way to the opportunities put in front of him. There is that side, but there is also the undoubted fact, that has to be taken into account in all our dealing with children, that they enter into a bodily condition that is tainted. They are burdened from the moment of conception by the hereditary qualities, the hereditary limitations, and the hereditary taints of their parents and ancestors. This seems just as true whether we express it in natural language, that of biological heredity and genetics; or whether we express it in a religious language, in terms of the notion of the "sins of the forefathers," the *amartima propatorikon*; or whether we speak of it in psychological language, say of Jung's collective unconscious, the atavistic memory of mankind. Whether it is an entirely natural, biological phenomenon, or whether it is an essential spiritual phenomenon connected with the will of man and the temptation and fall as described by Father Thwaites, or whether we look at it psychologically as something between the two, there is always the basic fact that the child, from the moment of conception, carries with it certain defects. The child has to overcome obstacles by the very fact of his having entered into a human body and having acquired that body from human parents. That seems to me to be common ground throughout all the different approaches to this problem. There is the entry of a spiritual being, with a spiritual consciousness, into a vessel of a body that is not spiritual and that is tainted by the conditions of human life into which that spiritual essence has entered. The problems that are created for us in our lives arise mainly from this duality of our nature — on the one hand spiritual, and on the other hand earthly.

Not very much was said in these lectures about the prenatal period, although I tried to emphasize this because my own experience has convinced me that many of the burdens connected with the spiritual hunger of children have already been laid on them by the time they are born, and have to be dealt with after their birth. It follows that there is no escaping from them unless the parents themselves — before and at the time of conception and during the whole period of gestation — live their lives in a state of purity of which very few of us are capable. As parents, we inevitably burden our children with taints, and put obstacles in front of them which they will have to overcome and with which we shall have to help them.

Then comes birth and the period from birth to the sixth, seventh, or eighth year. Dr. Montessori's direct scientific study and observation of children, carefully done with thousands of children, led her to regard the age of six or six and a half as the next transitional age. Adam Bittleston spoke of seven years as Steiner's dividing point. Pak Subuh speaks of eight years old as being the time of transition. Anyhow, somewhere between six and eight years old, the first cycle of life on the earth is finished, and the question we must ask is: What is it that is happening during those first six, seven, or eight years?

Obviously the child has been coming to terms with earthly life, with the natural order, with the world as brought to him through his senses. Then the question comes as to whether, during that period, there is also room for attention to spiritual problems. I think that everyone who spoke was in agreement that there is no room for an intellectual, mental approach during those years. There is nothing that can be taught with the mind, for the thinking mind cannot absorb abstract ideas until much later. There was a noticeable agreement throughout that something should be set in front of children during that time; whether it is through the spiritual essence of the natural world, as Adam Bittleston emphasized, or whether it is through the practice of prayer, as Father Thwaites recommended. Again, there are the means suggested by Mario Montessori on the basis of Maria Montessori's example. He suggested certain emblems or symbols of the spiritual life at home and in schools, such as a statue of the Blessed Virgin with a candle lit in front of it. The same idea came out in Mr. Polack's lecture which touched everyone so deeply. He drew the picture of the Jewish child and the contact he makes through his mother, who is the natural channel during those years for his contact with a sense of reality, in the lighting of the candles and the whole ritual of the Sabbath meal. Clearly in those cases — and I think it is probably true of all of the lectures — the suggestion is that we should put something before young children which will form for them a kind of symbol of the invisible world and not any mental image or explanation.

In the talks that I have about the Gurdjieff approach and Subud, I emphasized that both Gurdjieff and Pak Subuh have spoken of the need to avoid any kind of direct approach to religious instruction, or teaching children about religion, or God, or spirituality, until after puberty. At first I felt nervous that what I had said was out of line with what was said by the others, but in reading the lectures through carefully, I came to the conclusion that the common understanding throughout is really this: We must provide something which will appeal as a picture, as a sensual image, and not as an idea. Father Thwaites saw no objection to the child's prayer being very natural, like speaking to another human being. He was content that they should be, as we should say, anthropomorphic, making use of sensual images. The story he told of the little girl who said that when she goes to heaven, the first thing she will do would be to give God a good hug, at first gave me quite a shock, because I try always to divest myself entirely of all kinds of anthropomorphic and sensual images, which I feel have led us into so many difficulties. On thinking this over and reading again Father Thwaites' lecture, I concluded that this really amounts to nothing more than to offer to the child a picture which he will not really take for reality any more than he takes other pictures at this stage. This is possible because he has not developed the critical faculty, the ability to assert that a particular statement is true or false.

May I at this point speak of the connection between spirituality and faith. You might agree that faith could be called the direct consciousness of spiritual reality. There are, however, also indirect forms of faith. There is faith or trust in a person, and there is faith or belief that a statement is true. These different kinds of faith are discussed in Martin Buber's book, *Two Types of Faith.* We shall all agree that the second kind of indirect faith has no meaning for the young child; probably it has no meaning until after puberty when it suddenly becomes very important. For the young child, the first kind of faith must of necessity be intimately connected with his parents. Unless he trusts in his parents, he can scarcely be expected to trust in God, whom he is bound to picture in terms of a parent image. Hence comes Gurdjieff's saying, "For the young child the parents occupy the place of God; if he loves his father and mother, later on he will love God." But neither the anthropomorphic faith in a person nor the logical belief in spiritual truths correspond to the innate faith that Maria Montessori recognized in her children, and which aroused her own faith.

It seems therefore that the primary and essential

faith — which has neither object nor form, which is neither belief "in" nor belief "that" — is the one that matters. This is the faith that can be kept and transmitted from one stage in the child's development to another. Therefore we should not, in looking at the child and the problems of the child up to seven years old, concern ourselves very much with the validity of the particular images that are put in front of him. They serve to give him a taste of the connection between his own feeling for spiritual reality — which is the basic faith — and this sense-world that he has entered and must learn to live in and understand. As I see it, the various suggestions that have been made by the lecturers — of putting simple images, symbols, gestures, and particularly acts such as prayer — in front of children are all consistent with one another. The simplest picture of all was the one of Mario Montessori when he said that his mother "always had a statue of the Virgin near the child, standing illuminated by a small light. This is something that is different from the child's ordinary surroundings, and when the mother passes there, she makes the sign of the cross or some kind of acknowledgement." It was just the same in Mr. Polack's talk, with the Friday night and the mother and the Sabbath candles and so on. Something like that is common to all the different talks. This is not in any way concerned with the assent or rejection of any kind of doctrine, it is not a question of believing *that,* and therefore there is no need for concern because these forms and symbols may, from a more mature point of view, look invalid or even dangerous. But, of course, that problem does come with the later transition, to which I shall come in a moment, when the child enters the age of reason.

Next we come to one factor upon which we are all agreed: In dealing with children, it is ourselves for whom we are responsible. It is our own behavior that matters, not the behavior of the children. It is whether we are really seeking to perfect ourselves and to liberate ourselves from the defects of our own nature that matters, and also our own sincerity and our own ability to admit and not to hide in any way from children our own mistakes and defects. These are the things that create the necessary confidence during the first seven years. Mario Montessori described the child who was told not to tell lies and then heard his mother on the telephone inventing a migraine to keep an aunt from coming to tea. When he saw that his mother had her hat on and was ready to go out, the child burst into tears and said, "You have lied, you have no migraine." This picture was repeated in one or another form in several lectures. I think all of us who have had dealings with children have seen the terrible emotional shock that comes when they see that their parents, or other adults, are not what they pretend to be. It seems to me that the only way of protecting children from that shock is not to pretend to be anything. Providing we can keep ourselves free all the time from pretending to be something in front of children, we avert a certain shock which tends to close in them an inner door. It cuts them off from the confidence which will be needed when they enter into the second period, which begins somewhere between the sixth and the eighth year and goes on to somewhat after puberty.

There is no doubt that sometime between the ages of six and eight there comes a great change, and that during this next period learning in the true sense of the word begins to be possible. There is not merely the interest in objects as objects, but the interest in relationships, and therefore the relationships between things and between people. They begin to be able to learn and in the sense of ordinary, straightforward education the potential of these years is probably still not grasped by educators. Experiments have recently been made, both in the United States and the Soviet Union, showing that practically everything that needs to be learned in the way of facts, languages, mathematical operations, physics, chemistry, and so on can be taught quite effectively between seven and fourteen years, providing the particular psychological characteristics of these years are taken into account. Now whether or not this is a good thing I am not prepared to say; it may even be a very bad thing. The intensive exploitation of the capacity for learning that exists between seven and fourteen years may have disastrous results later on. But the very fact that such experiments have been made, and have shown it is possible in a matter of weeks for an eight year old to assimilate mathematical techniques that normally are not taught until the age of fifteen and sixteen and later, demonstrates the extraordinary potential latent in the psyche of the child from the age of seven or eight onwards. Clearly, the same procedure could not be followed until this transition has come.

The question then arises as to the spiritual problem and what is to be done about it during these years. Mario Montessori suggested that the sense of obligation begins to appear at this age, and that it is possible to teach the commandments and the nature of our responsibilities in our human relationships. My own view is that the sense of obligation is not fully awakened at the age of seven or eight, but that it is growing and developing during the years from seven to fourteen. It comes into full flower — and sometimes with explosive force — at the time of puberty. The "Garden of Eden" period of life, the naked period, a kind of "Adam" period, lasts from birth to seven years old. The period from seven or eight years onward is something quite different. After the transition, the important thing from the spiritual point of view is probably (here I am speaking partly from what Mr. Bittleston said, and partly from what Mario Montessori said) a faith in, not a belief that. It is the kind of faith that is nearer to trust, the first of Martin Buber's two kinds of faith, the kind of faith that is exemplified in Abraham, who put his trust in the Lord. Certainly at no stage in the story of Abraham from the beginning to the end is there the slightest indication that he had any sort of dogmatic faith, that he believed in anything like a creed. He simply trusted in God and led his life on the basis of a trust in God that was clearly — as we should now call it — anthropomorphic.

This will help us to distinguish three stages of faith. The very young child has direct, immediate faith: It is not "trust in" or "belief that." He trusts all and believes all; because, as Mario Montessori said, he is immersed in the spiritual reality. This immediate, interior faith has to come to terms with the mediate, outward experience of earthly life. It then turns into "trust in" his parents together, aided by the link forged by images, symbols, and acts of piety. The years from birth to seven or eight are, or should be, the age of trust.

In the second period, the child comes to terms with the wider situation. His vision is opening from the particular to the general, from direct experience to embrace the content of memory, thought, and imagination. With this comes a gradual transformation of faith from trust to belief. The spiritual reality is no longer directly experienced all the time, but only at increasingly rare intervals in moments of release or awakening of the obvious. It will tend to substitute an external image or idea for the direct experience. Faith will degenerate into "belief that."

This does not mean that no spiritual training is useful. On the contrary, there are acts which sustain and transform the simple inward faith. These acts have been variously described by our speakers. Mr. Polack and Father Thwaites laid stress upon the acts of worship that are available. There was the child who asked, "Please, Daddy, can I fast this year?" This illustrates the nature of the spiritual hunger: It is the need to act rightly, to act as the parents act. Several speakers have suggested that specific, visible acts of worship are not necessary. The child will observe and sense the parents' acceptance of obligations: He will wish to be "good" as his parents are good. He will accept that he has not reached the age when he can be taught the mysteries of faith. As Pak Subuh puts it, his parents worship for him and he worships through them.

The reality of faith is experienced as an act, not as idea or belief. That is why it is so important that "faith as trust" should be carried over from the first period to the second. The tragedy is that so often this trust is not maintained. Perhaps the greater part of the avoidable troubles, the psychic troubles of life, and the inability to recapture the awareness of spiritual reality spring from this: Trust has been betrayed.

This comes in part because of the conflict between home and school. It arises acutely if there is conflict between father and mother. It comes if there is conflict between theory and practice, between precept and example. Wherever there is conflict of these kinds, trust is shaken. With the shaking of trust, there comes a closing up, and when the age of puberty is reached the child no longer trusts in anyone or anything.

Our Quaker speaker, Mr. Williams, said that he found nothing to be distressed about in the feeling of revolt and rejection that arises among young people after puberty. They should not be expected to conform for they belong to the house of the future, or they are the house of the future, into which we are not able to enter. Therefore we must respect their house and remember that they, like us, yearn to sing the "Lord's Song in a Strange Land," and we can feel confident that they will find it — if only we put our own house in order.

You will remember that Father Thwaites referred to the frequency with which, in our modern world, children after puberty — or more exactly, after leaving — abandon the regular practice of prayer and church worship. Mr. Polack also referred to the lapse into irreligion of Jewish children, even from homes where the law is more or less strictly kept. Here we are faced with "The Spiritual Hunger of the Modern Child," and are coming to the point where we have to consider the various solutions that have been offered to the problem it presents.

It seems to me there is no necessity for the condition of revolt. The real problems that arise afterwards need not be of this kind that are due to lack of trust. The true problems arise from the awakening of a different need. They are connected with the need to participate, to share, to feel oneself part of a greater whole. They are the spiritual aspect of what, on the psychic level, is the social problem of integration into the human body corporate. Mario Montessori gave the example of the boys who had been at a school where they were supposed to be backward and difficult; but where, thanks to the right handling, the boys had attained a normal outlook. After puberty they spontaneously began to wish to take care of older people, to take on the task of visiting people who were lonely. Mr. Montessori looks upon that period as the time when human responsibilities begin to be accepted and when right and wrong come to be understood in terms of a larger context. The problem of the meaning of life that expresses itself in questions such as, "Why am I here? What is my life for?" should be faced in an atmosphere of trust. The child should have gone through the Abraham period without having lost the childlike qualities of Abraham's faith — faith in God as a person — and come into the other stage of believing in certain truths, believing that there are laws, accepting the laws of right and wrong as true, accepting certain statements as false, and so on. That is the second kind of faith, but it is no longer isolated from the total experience of life as so often happens when there has been an attempt to instill religious or spiritual dogmas. In this way, the satisfaction of spiritual hunger comes from the immediate faith that includes and sustains both the faith that believes in God

as a person and the faith that believes that the teaching
of religion is true. The underlying belief is then not directed towards any object, not even a divine object: It
is formless faith without content. This is an indescribable
condition, but it is one that we can recognize as possible
at all stages of childhood. This faith does not depend
upon some particular form, or person, or doctrine, or
image of any kind; but just believes. It is the true foundation of spirituality as it has been presented to us in
these lectures: that life makes sense, that there is Goodness, that there is Truth and Love, and that these things
are both human and superhuman. When one has said that,
one has perhaps already said too much, because one has
expressed in words what was much more true before it
was put into words. It does not require any mental
images, since it is the underlying conviction.

I think there is something here that can be watched and
that really matters. We dare not speak to children about
it because if we do, we shall reduce it to one of the other
two, more limited kinds of faith. The real center of spiritual hunger is the need for the assurance that there is a
divine order, that I have my place in that order and that
the divine reality is good towards me as I must be good
towards it. All this has to be transformed stage by stage
from the faith of the very young child that is pure
spiritual awareness, to the informed faith that establishes
the full religious life of the mature man or woman.

When I was thinking about that question earlier, of
teaching children about God, the words of the Lord's
Prayer came into my mind. In the first sentence, with
its three phrases, "Our Father, which art in heaven,
hallowed be thy name," we can recognize the spiritual
attitudes towards which we are directed. The first is
the Fatherhood of God; that is, the sense of a relationship which is reciprocal. The Father is not a father without children, so that God needs us as much as we need
him or he would not be a Father. The second phrase re-

minds us that He is in heaven. This certainly means the invisible, spiritual world. It reminds us that this reality is out of reach of our senses. This is made explicit by the phrase, "Hallowed be thy name." We cannot approach God himself, only his name. This reminds us that we cannot know, we can only name. That is why it does not really matter that we should tell children this, that, or the other about God. Whatever we may say, we are only talking to them about names. We are not talking to them about God, because that we cannot do.

Only, it is rather dangerous if we begin to suppose that we are talking about God when we are only talking about the name of God. We must not imagine that we are showing God when we are only presenting an image or picture. One of my earliest memories as a child illustrates this point. I was a tiny baby when my mother took me to Florence. We lived behind the Boboli Gardens near the Pitti Gallery. I can remember clearly the picture of God the Father by Giotto that was then in the Pitti Gallery. I don't think I was more than a year and a half when I came away, and yet I remember this picture of God with his great beard blowing out in every direction to the limits of the canvas. I went back many years later to Florence and I had to go and see this picture of God the Father by Giotto in order to come to terms with the image or picture of God that my Italian nurse had put in front of me by bringing me to the Pitti Gallery and saying, "Ecco Dio Padre."

We must remember that children can have put in front of them images of this sort which can be dangerously persistent and be taken for the reality. I feel that we may safely do all these things — especially when they are in the form of gestures, such as showing a statue of the Blessed Virgin with a lighted candle and crossing oneself. The danger comes when one begins to *tell* children things: "This is God," or "That is heaven," or "That is the spiritual reality," and so on. There is a danger that later on these images will remain as truths which must be believed. What may be valid for the age of trust ceases to be valid for the age of reason, when the truth or falsehood of propositions begins to have a meaning. I feel we should bear in mind that this does run through what has been said during these lectures. We can use various images in the early stages to preserve the connection for the children between the natural and the supernatural. This is quite all right so long as there is not formed in the child the notion of truth and falsity, of logical statements. We must not expect that children, before the age of puberty, can grasp the nature of the "truth value of a proposition," as logicians call it. That is not how they approach their problem, and what we call lies in children very often are not lies at all.

I am just digressing at the moment. It is strange that the child should really be distressed at her mother saying that she had a headache when she had not, and yet tell a story of having seen a gypsy come into the gardens and sell her this or that when it was nothing but a fairy tale. These are quite different things. There is no doubt that the kind of truth required by young children is not truth in the sense of true propositions, but trustworthiness, and that is where the distinction lies. If we are sufficiently concerned with trustworthiness, we shall pass through that period safely. During the next period, there is an immense amount to be understood and learned by children about the natural order. Between the ages of seven and fourteen, they can come to feel the reality of the spiritual world through their human relationships. They acquire a sense of duty and of right and wrong. Later, in the next stage, they awaken to the need to serve, the need to find a place, to belong to the divine order of creation, to give and to take. I think that these will enable us to do the part that falls to us as far as the transformation of faith in the child is concerned.

There are no doubt many things I intended to refer to

in the nine lectures in order to bring out adequately the other viewpoints. I am just not going to try now, as I much sooner would spend the next half-hour or forty minutes in talking with you and getting you to say what you think about all this and for me to make my comments. I only hope that what I have said has not been altogether too incoherent.

QUESTIONS

Q. I did not hear all the other lectures, so I do not know if the question of small children learning from prayer came up?

Mr. Bennett: Yes, it came out very strongly last week. The core of Father Thwaites' lecture was that prayer alone matters, and that by teaching children to pray we shall put them under divine protection. He also said it did not matter that the children's prayers might be naive, that they might not understand, and that as long as you teach a child to pray, everything else will come right. I think that it was only in this lecture that the emphasis was put so entirely on prayer as the instrument of spiritual development.

Q. I suppose Gurdjieff would say no, not with a small child?

Mr. Bennett: Gurdjieff distinguished between prayer that is mechanical — whether of the mind or the heart — and prayer that is conscious. The child is not ready for conscious prayer. Last week Father Thwaites was asked to comment on the question of the mother who asked whether or not she should teach her child to pray. I had answered, "If you believe in prayer, teach your child to pray; if you do not believe, you cannot teach your child to pray." Father Thwaites said exactly the same: If a mother does not believe, then she cannot teach her child to pray. It is better, he said, to find somebody else to teach the child, or to set to work to find out for herself.

It did occur to me that this leaves the question rather in the air. As someone said in the course of the discussion last week, there are so few people in the world — in our Western world especially — who have any definite spiritual experience which enables them to confim for themselves the reality of prayer and its objective significance. The question was put whether it is really possible for anyone who lacks spiritual experience to teach children to pray. Father Thwaites said, and I must say I agree with him, that it is not necessary that the mother should have such a spiritual life that she has a direct kind of mystical insight in the efficacy of prayer. It is sufficient that she should really be satisfied in herself that prayer is right and good.

If one can recognize even a little of the formless faith of which I have just spoken, then from that, prayer can be taught. One may not believe any dogmatic proposition at all, or one may not have any particular trust in any church; but if one has that foundation, which is the formless faith, the rest will come. Prayer itself will be transformed from mechanical repetition to conscious participation in the spiritual reality.

Q. I was taught to pray when I was little, and I should be sorry for any small child who has to go through anything without it.

Q. I would like to point out that I have never been taught to pray at all, and find this whole discussion either completely above my head or meaningless. But I certainly recognize this quality of the third kind of faith, which cannot be put into words. I am very grateful that never in my education have I been given any kind of anthropomorphic image, because that would have misled me completely, I am sure. I feel very strongly about this point.

Mr. Bennett: I feel that here we are in front of something where probably there is a certain divergence between our lecturers. The basic question is, "How is it possible, without spoiling something, to make the transition from a kind of natural presentation of spiritual reality, which is the only one possible in the first seven years? That is all the young child has contact with: The bodily powers, the senses, and so on are the only avenue the child has to a religious life. If we have taught too much during the early phases, it seems to me there is a danger that this will persist, and there will be a problem to get it out of the system — as I had the problem of getting Giotto's "God the Father" out of my system. If there has been prudent instruction in religious or spiritual matters — for instance, teaching the Ten Commandments — all will go well enough from seven to fourteen. But after that all sorts of questions arise, such as: "But the world in which we live is not like the spiritual world I have been taught about." Then come all Mr. Williams' questions of revolt and the problems of puberty. It does seem to me that what I said can be put into some practical form. That is, that one should be very careful that there should remain a certain element of, I would say "playfulness," about this with the young child. If religious instruction is made too obvious, there can arise a kind of terror. Many people have told me how they have been brought up as Roman Catholics, with real terror of mortal sin, because at the age of four or five they were already told that mortal sin will bring them to hell. Clearly something has gone wrong, because the Church's teaching about mortal sin is not terrifying at all.

An extreme example was given last week of the young mother in the maternity ward who would not feed her child because he had not been baptized and therefore was wicked. Father Thwaites assured us that this was an utterly absurd travesty of the reality. You must understand that these kinds of things do happen, not only to

Catholic children, but also to Protestant, or Jewish, or Buddhist children. The same thing can happen anywhere if everything is taken too seriously and too heavily. If we are going to take a natural approach, making a natural link between the spiritual, inner consciousness and the outer, sensual consciousness, we have to be very gentle in handling it.

If you speak, let us say, about mortal sin to a child of five years old, and hell as a place to which you will certainly go if you are in mortal sin, he or she will take this picture literally and it will leave behind terrible causes of suffering and possibly revolt against religion itself. Similarly, if you show a child pictures of God the Father with a great beard, this inevitably will remain if it is taken too seriously. But if one can believe that sometimes God may shave, a child may be a good deal more comforted by this, because God with such a big beard would be very terrifying. At least it was to me. And therefore I say that if it is realized that pictures and symbols are useful, but must not be treated too seriously, all will be well. Children must not be treated as if they were already able to see the common sense significance of images. Then you get into trouble.

As the child approaches puberty, there is no doubt that we must make sure that he is made aware of all the hazards of life, the departures from law, the fact that the commandments are not kept, the fact that we can cut ourselves off from God, and so on. He must learn to accept that human beings are not the moral beings that they should be according to the rules. During that period, this must be kept sufficiently alive so that when they do come to meet the reality of things, it will not produce the second kind of shock. There is the possibility of avoiding the anthropomorphism, the naturalism of religious instruction and of leaving it so that the inner consciousness will develop, trusting that there will be a spiritual recognition of spiritual truths.

That is a matter that I regard as open, and I believe that we shall not be able to continue in the future, with the progress of scientific knowlege which will require that children between seven and fourteen years should learn a great deal more about the world than they did in the past. I do not believe that we can continue to teach them about spiritual matters in the same sort of naive way that we did in the past. This has got to be faced by religious people and by educators and parents. Something has got to be done.

Q.   Following on from this point, the most significant thing that I can remember about the early stages is the feeling of living in a family which was creatively oriented. Looking back in a more mature light on those years, this was the one thing that was important; not what was said, nor the fact that there was any possible suggestion. I must say that my parents were anti-religious, and at the same time there was a sense of meaning and creativity, and of the obligation of service in the kind of life that they were leading. This to me was the important thing, because it meant that I was not misled by any sort of false image about the meaning of religion, and was able later on to come without preconceived ideas to the awareness of spiritual realities.

Mr. Bennett: Yes, I am sure that this is true, and if I have not said much about the family it is not because the family is not the center, but because it is evident to all of us that the family is the key to the spiritual life of children. There is no substitute for the family, and there never can be. Nevertheless, the family requires a certain harmony. If there are serious conflicts between the parents they will be transmitted to the children. It will be nearly as bad if there are conflicts between the parents and the outer world, especially the school. But where there is a sense, as you say, of service, that life is for fulfillment of some task, the family can be a very big help. Your father is a schoolmaster; anyone who is a dedicated teacher of children is inevitably carried outside of the egoism that infects the ordinary life of people.

Q. Could you express your personal opinion as to who you think ought to give the main teaching to children on religious or spiritual matters, especially up to the age of eight. The parents? In particular, the father or the mother? Or should it be an outside religious teacher, whether it is the local vicar, or a schoolteacher, or anyone with religious authority?

Mr. Bennett: Oh yes. If something has to be shown or said during those years, it is the mother who should do it. That does not mean, of course, that the father has no role to play; he has a very great role indeed, because he should be the foundation of trust. I would like to mention what Gurdjieff said about this particular thing. The important thing for children is love of their parents. He used to say, "A child who does not love its parents will not be able to love God; so long as the parents are alive, they occupy the place of God. If that place is rightly prepared, when the parents die, God will enter it." This was a constant theme of his, and he said that this love must be for both the parents, and that it is their duty to see that it is fostered at all times. The father should direct the children towards the mother and the mother should direct the children towards the father. Not the mother trying to attract one or another of the children to herself, but on the contrary, the mother should constantly be engaged in strengthening the bond between the children and the father, and the father constantly engaged in strengthening the bond between the children and the mother. This is the procedure which, I am very ashamed to say, I forgot to mention in the lecture that I gave on this, because it is one of the central elements of Gurdjieff's approach to children. It certainly does not mean that the child up to the age of seven or eight has nothing to receive from his father, but that the mother is the more direct channel.

Q. There is a saying, "Give us the child between the age

of three and the age of eight, and after that no one will be able to alter him, or alter what we have taught him." So it should really be a joint venture of father and mother?

Mr. Bennett: It will be a joint venture of father and mother. If we speak of what is ideal, the father and mother are one in any case, and therefore nothing that the mother does will be other than the father's, and nothing that the father does will be separated from the mother. Father and mother are ideally one in body and soul. Any departure from this ideal has to be compensated for. For example, if one of the parents has died, or is not able for some reason to perform his or her true function as a parent, the other should not take the whole burden on himself or herself. The creation of a spiritual environment is, in its essence, a joint action. It should not be attempted, therefore, by a solitary parent. The roles are not interchangeable; the role of the mother is different from the role of the father. Later, between the ages of seven and fourteen, the role of the father begins to be more and more significant. I do not think this is different with boys and girls. You should bear in mind that in all religions the need for godparents is recognized. It seems that there is not a complete spiritual environment unless there is an element from outside the family. In our time, the role of godparents has become an empty formality. This is typical of the failure of our modern world to appreciate the significance of ancient customs. There is a real need for the intervention of a friend — who is neither parent nor priest — to convey to the child certain notions of spirituality during the period from seven years to puberty.

The role of the priest should be less intimate. I would say that he should remain as a symbol of the spiritual reality, and not the creator of the spiritual atmosphere or environment. There are, of course, many modern parents who are not connected closely with any church and yet feel strongly the need to satisfy the spiritual hunger of their children.

As for schools, I should be treading on very dangerous ground in expressing an opinion as to the value of a denominational as against a non-denominational school. But I would like to say that in the last few days a sincere, practising Catholic told me that he was convinced that he had kept his loyalty to his church precisely because he was sent to a non-Catholic school. I am inclined to think that most of us would agree that the revolt against religion is far more likely to occur where too much has been taught rather than where there has been no religious instruction at all.

Q. I do see the importance of not losing our children's trust from the age of seven onwards. My mother was always very backward in talking about matters of sex. This created very great difficulties in my relationship with her.

Mr. Bennett: To tell the truth, I had forgotten about sex! It is quite true that sex and instruction about sex have often come up in these lectures. Mr. Williams strongly emphasized the obligation of parents. Last week, I noticed that Father Thwaites mentioned, as one of the three main planks on which a normal spiritual life is to be built, an adequate and early teaching about sex.

I do know that if this obligation is neglected by parents, it does tend to break down the relationship of trust. In my opinion, the earlier it is done the better. It is essential that all this be quite clear to children before puberty so that there is no false mystery in puberty for them. Of course there is always a mystery, but I mean nothing odd or secret about it. The earlier children learn about the significance and physiology of sex, the less it astonishes them and shocks them, and the more easily they take it all for granted. The necessary progressive additions can be explained to them so that they can deal with problems as they arise — whether it is problems of their own bodies or those of the behavior of other children — in a straightforward and simple manner. It is one of the tragedies of recent generations that children were made to feel that there is something shameful about sex. Now it goes too much the other way.

Q. Father Thwaites said that children ought to be taught to pray as soon as possible. Could you give us some idea of what you consider the best way of moving on from the "talking to Jesus" kind of prayer to the formless prayer, such as we find in the meditation of the Vedanta?

Mr. Bennett: I do think that prayer is of inestimable value, but I could not feel the way that Father Thwaites obviously does feel about it when he spoke last week. This is because I have a dread of the "hangover" of what you call the "talking to Jesus." He himself spoke of the tragedy of the number of children, well brought up in Catholic homes, who cease to follow their worship after school time. Mr. Polack also said it must be admitted to be true of Jewish children. I think that everyone knows that this is true throughout the world and that this comes just as much with children who have been taught from childhood to pray regularly as with those whose prayer has been neglected. Therefore it seems to me that there is something more here that has to be faced: If there is to be prayer, and I think it is right that there should be, there must also be the transition in prayer corresponding to the transitions in the child's nature. If this is not provided for sufficiently, if nothing is done to go from the "talking to Jesus" kind of prayer to another kind of prayer which is really appropriate from the age of seven to fourteen, and on again to the more meditative prayer which is really required after the age of puberty, then we may do more harm than good. I feel that this is one of the things that has not been adequately dealt with in this series of lectures, but I am very glad you have spoken about it because it has brought home to me the need to come to terms with this problem. I intend to do a certain amount of reading about it myself, because I am not clear what the general practice is on this point. It seems evident to me that prayer must change as the child changes. As all other faculties and powers begin to change in passing through these different fundamental periods, clearly there should be a change in the form of the experience of the presence of God.

I do not feel competent at this moment to say more than that. I feel very certain that there should be some guidance given to people — to parents especially — who want to approach this in a realistic way corresponding to our present time, as to what they should do when the "talking to Jesus" kind of period is passed and the children enter into the period when prayer should have a more serious content. It seems very probable, from all that has been said, that a serious readjustment has to be made. We are living in an age when religious anthropomorphism is unacceptable to the majority of educated people. This emphatically does not mean that they turn away from religion or that they will not accept the statement of faith embodied in the creed, but they cannot accept an interpretation that treats God as if he were a superman. No difficulty should arise if children are helped during the years from seven to fourteen to divest themselves of the anthropomorphic images of childhood and to take on a more reverent attitude towards the mystery of faith.

Q. I am a Catholic, but I was brought up in a very unorthodox way. My mother was a Protestant and my father was away. My mother taught me to pray, and I loved it. I still do. I was confirmed at twelve; the sacraments were give to me at the right time. As someone said earlier, having none was right for him. So my way was good for me. If parents could give it to children at the right ages, it would work out all right.

Mr. Bennett: This is what I mean when I say there

should be a transition from this simple kind of natural prayer, like speaking to a person, to something which has content — like the ritual, like the sacramental worship. All of this is given to children in the Catholic Church. But then the question arises: What happens later on?

Q.   Mario Montessori spoke of silence. Once when a child said to a Montessori teacher, "Is God in heaven?" she said, "No, God is in the silence." This is a good foundation for meditative prayer.

Mr. Bennett: I think that is very true. I remember when I was first taken to a Montessori school — I think it must have been in 1921 — I was very impressed by the silence of the children. It was at Plaistow, at a very rough place with very rough children. I could not believe that it could be possible that they should all become silent like this. When they say, "Is God in heaven?" it is possible to say, "This silence gives you an idea of what heaven is like." Children's silence in that way is one of the most heavenly things that one can find on earth.

Q.   For those who have adolescent children, try reading tonight the first lines of Samuel Taylor Coleridge's *The Pains of Sleep.* It is almost perfect.

THE JOHN G. BENNETT TAPES

These tapes hold a message for everyone who believes that our society is approaching a point of crises.

They are cassette recordings of talks given at Sherborne House by John G. Bennett during the five experimental one-year courses he conducted there.

In common with many modern thinkers, Bennett believed that man was not fulfilling his obligations to the earth and to his destiny; but unlike many he believed that this could be remedied.

Bennett had a remarkable ability to transmit the most complex ideas in his lectures with consiseness and clarity. His unique way of thinking was often demonstrated in exactly how he said something, as well as in what he said.

Many of the themes are taken from the ideas of G.I. Gurdjieff, expanded and developed by Bennett's own unique and original studies.

A list of over forty of these tapes is available from Claymont Communications.

CLAYMONT COMMUNICATIONS

Claymont Communications was established in 1978 by the Claymont Society to publish and distribute books, tapes and related materials concerning the Work. We carry titles by many authors and offer a wide range of works by J.G. Bennett. For a copy of our latest list write to:

Claymont Communications
P.O. Box 926, Charles Town
W. Va. 25414